A MULTICULTURAL APPROACH TO PHYSICAL EDUCATION

Proven Strategies for Middle and High School

Rhonda L. Clements, EdD
Hofstra University
Hempstead, New York

Suzanne K. Kinzler, MS
Queens Gateway to the Health Sciences Secondary School
Jamaica, New York

Human Kinetics

Library of Congress Cataloging-in-Publication Data

Clements, Rhonda L.
A multicultural approach to physical education : proven strategies for middle and high school / Rhonda L. Clements, Suzanne K. Kinzler.
p. cm.
Includes bibliographical references.
ISBN 0-7360-3882-5 (softcover)
1. Physical education and training--Study and teaching (Secondary) 2. Multicultural education. I. Kinzler, Suzanne K., 1962-II. Title.
GV363 .C49 2002
613.7'071'2--dc21

2002007774

Acquisitions Editors: Amy N. Clocksin and Scott Wikgren; **Developmental Editor:** Jennifer Clark; **Assistant Editor:** Amanda Gunn; **Copyeditor:** Jennifer L. Davis; **Graphic Designer:** Karen O'Sullivan; **Graphic Artists:** Karen O'Sullivan and Dawn Sills; **Photo Manager:** Leslie A. Woodrum; **Cover Designer:** Keith Blomberg; **Photographer (cover):** Leslie A. Woodrum; **Photographers (interior):** Suzanne K. Kinzler and Andrea Petruzzi; **Illustrator:** G.H.C. Illustrations; **Printer:** Versa Press

Printed in the United States of America
10 9 8 7 6 5 4 3 2 1

Human Kinetics
Web site: www.HumanKinetics.com

United States: Human Kinetics
P.O. Box 5076
Champaign, IL 61825-5076
800-747-4457
e-mail: humank@hkusa.com

Canada: Human Kinetics
475 Devonshire Road Unit 100
Windsor, ON N8Y 2L5
800-465-7301 (in Canada only)
e-mail: orders@hkcanada.com

Europe: Human Kinetics
107 Bradford Road
Stanningley
Leeds LS28 6AT, United Kingdom
+44 (0) 113 255 5665
e-mail: hk@hkeurope.com

Australia: Human Kinetics
57A Price Avenue
Lower Mitcham, South Australia 5062
08 8277 1555
e-mail: liahka@senet.com.au

New Zealand: Human Kinetics
P.O. Box 105-231
Auckland Central
09-523-3462
e-mail: hkp@ihug.co.nz

CONTENTS

ACTIVITY FINDER

ACTIVITY FINDER

Title of Activity	Corresponding Country	Multicultural Outcome	Page
Chicago Softball	USA	Conform to group needs	87
Three Team Softball	USA	Reflect upon the importance of collaboration	88
Collective Softball	USA	Create opportunities for success	89
Finnish Baseball (Pesapallo)	Finland	Engage in new playing skills	90
Ready Or Not Ring Hockey	France	Adhere to rules	92
African Bolo Ball	Africa	Adapt to physical limitations	94
Sweep Me Away Broomball	Canada	Analyze playing positions	95
Egyptian Group Bowling	Egypt	Interpret results for group efforts	97
Pigskin Pass	USA	Practice patience	98
Six Minute Touchdown	USA	Promote teamwork	99
Try Harder Handball	Greece	Negotiate playing positions	101
Checkmate Handball	China	Maintain motivation	103
Unlimited Pass Volleyball	USA	Become empowered	105
Fantastic Fistball	Germany	Verbalize strategies	107
Stickball	England	Compare methods of skill execution	109
Hit the Stick	England	Discover ways of performing	111
Quick Action Basketball	USA	Seek help from group	112
Korfball	Holland	Propose alternative rules	114
Four Season Ball	International	Develop group strategies	116
Run Away Rounders	England	Celebrate peaceful competition	117
Almost Ultimate	USA	Increase group endurance	119
Four Target Frisbee	USA	Share responsibility	121
Team Deck Tennis	England	Accept new challenges	123
Culturally Diverse Really Wild Relays	International	Identify strengths and talents	125
Team Rock, Paper, Scissors	Japan	Play for luck and chance	127
Trades	Netherlands	Adjust to different situations	129
Toss and Catch Nets	Philippines	Behave autonomously	131
Horse Race	England	Describe group conduct	132
Japanese Group Combative Challenges	Japan	Contribute to group efforts	134
Awesome Archway	France	Foster a sense of interdependence	136
All Wet Sport Acquatico	Italy	Accommodate group needs	137
Rescue Me Aquatic Relays	Japan	Provide or respect leadership	139
Kickboard Water Polo	England	Value perseverance	140
American Indian Dodge and Throw	USA	Show concern for others	141
All Sport Novelty Meets	USA	Perform one's own special talents	143

ACKNOWLEDGMENTS

The authors are deeply indebted to the many physical educators and their school's administrations who field-tested the contents of this book:

- Queens Gateway School to the Health Sciences, Queens, NY
- Dewitt Clinton High School, South Bronx, NY
- Flushing High School, Queens, NY
- Hempstead High School, Hempstead, NY
- Roosevelt High School, Roosevelt, NY
- Berkley Carroll High School, Brooklyn, NY
- New Visions for Public School, New York, NY
- Marte Valle Secondary School, New York, NY
- Wadleigh School, New York, NY
- Paul Robeson High School, Brooklyn, NY
- Mark Hopkins Middle School, Brooklyn, NY
- St. Martin De Porres, Uniondale, NY
- Park West High School, New York, NY
- Rippowani Cisqua School, Bedford, NY

Additional thanks are extended to Dr. Lenard Wechsler, Dr. Joanne Dusel, and the World Council Members of The International Association for the Child's Right To Play (IPA) for their invaluable suggestions and expertise in sports and games played throughout the world. Recognition is given to Karen O'Sullivan for her graphic art in the sport formations, G.H.C. Illustrations, and photographer Andrea Petruzzi.

Acknowledgment is gladly given to The New York City Board of Education and Take The Field, Inc. for their willingness and financial support in the on-going implementation of this project.

INTRODUCTION

This resource offers a multicultural approach to physical education for students in grades seven through twelve. The approach was found to increase the individual's feelings of self-worth and generated a shared sense of accomplishment among students of varied cultural and economic backgrounds. It also offers a variety of innovative learning experiences aimed at fostering interpersonal relationships through physical activity. The contents are based on the results of a ten-year curriculum development project involving students from several metropolitan and urban high schools. Experienced physical educators field-tested the approach or supervised graduate students who implemented and assessed the results of this resource's contents. None of the contents require elaborate equipment or expansive playing facilities and can be used in class sizes exceeding 35 students.

We have organized this resource into six distinctive chapters to assist the reader's implementation process. An Activity Finder is included that identifies the name of the activity, the corresponding country, the multicultural outcome, and the page where the activity is located.

Chapter 1, *The Use of a Multicultural Approach,* describes the recommended approach and identifies the use of student learning outcomes that reflect multicultural education.

Chapter 2, *The Use of a Simplified Lesson Format and Multicultural Outcomes,* describes the elements reflected in this text's multicultural approach and shows how they can occur within a simplified lesson format. This format is consistently used throughout the text, and was found to be an effective means to assist the teacher's planning, organization, and presentation of content.

Chapter 3, *Activities for Increased Individual Interaction,* provides the reader with 30 partner activities in which the student can discover exceptional physical abilities through cooperative tasks and vigorous physical challenges. Increased self-worth is also achieved through a variety of leisure and fitness activities enjoyed by other cultures. Still other partner activities allow for individual strengths and talents to emerge in combative tasks and activities reflecting an enriched lifestyle. Many partner activities also provide opportunities for the individual to exhibit critical thinking and decision making by participating in numerous measurement tasks, the construction of modified sport equipment, completing creative worksheets, and through record keeping assignments involving individualized fitness workouts.

Chapter 4, *Activities for Increased Group Interaction,* contains 50 learning experiences aimed at groups of students developing a shared sense of pride and accomplishment. This is possible when students take part in lessons reflecting artistic dance forms and popular sports in the USA, as well as a variety of multicultural sports unknown to many students. Among others, these include street games, reflecting particular neighborhoods and ethnic groups in the USA, and modified versions of national sports, such as Finnish Baseball, that are unique to specific countries or areas of the world. Activities of this nature expand the group's appreciation of sports common to the American culture, and assist students in identifying differences in movement and sport activities from other cultures. Collective achievement is emphasized.

Chapter 5, *Assessing Multicultural Outcomes,* identifies three sample rubrics that can be used to determine the extent to which multicultural outcomes are achieved within a physical domain.

Chapter 6, *Additional Curriculum Considerations,* contains a variety of ideas and techniques to enhance the student's learning environment. All presented techniques reinforce a multicultural approach to learning.

An in-depth bibliography is included to ease the teacher's implementation process and search for additional literature.

Finally, it is the authors' hope that the information presented throughout this book will assist middle and high school physical educators in creating learning environments where all students will be motivated to learn from each other as they learn more about themselves.

PART I
TEACHING STRATEGIES

The Use of a Multicultural Approach

"We do not see things as they are; we see things as we are."
– Talmud

MULTICULTURAL EDUCATION is a very complex concept having numerous definitions and interpretations depending on an individual's previous experiences, opinions, and desired goals. Following an extensive review of classroom literature and discussions with experienced teachers and scholars in the field, it was determined that multicultural education should not be viewed as a teaching unit, a subject, or a topic reflecting special interest groups. Field-testing the concept within physical education settings showed that it is more than individuals learning about other cultures or developing an appreciation for one's heritage. Nor is it merely groups of students participating in a series of games and stretching exercises from other countries or understanding how to manipulate a piece of sport equipment from another nation. While these actions do spark student interest in multicultural settings, they do not necessarily enhance the individual's feeling of self-worth or positive attitudes toward others.

For the purpose of this book, the key to successful implementation was found in the word *education,* which emphasizes an on-going process. Therefore, based on the literature, a decision was made that multicultural education in middle and high school physical education is best infused throughout the curriculum in the form of an approach to teaching. Furthermore, student learning outcomes are more readily achieved when teachers plan lessons that convey goals or actions common to multicultural education, and are willing to expand their selection of activities in the existing curriculum. The expected change in student behavior when a multicultural approach is utilized is "how can I become involved?" instead of the more usual question of "what do I have to do today?"

THE TEACHER'S IMPLEMENTATION PROCESS FOR THE INDIVIDUAL

Proponents of multicultural education recognize that society depends on collective achievement. This understanding begins with the individual interacting positively with one other peer. As the individual learns more about his or her talents and physical abilities, worries of failure decrease, and there is an increased awareness of how he or she can contribute to partner and group efforts.

In Step One of the teacher's implementation process for the individual, the teacher plays a critical role in awakening the student's self-awareness and social consciousness by selecting a multicultural outcome aimed at individual or partner interaction and increased feelings of self-worth. Feelings of self-worth are often lacking in students in metropolitan schools having substantial class sizes and large minority populations, yet self-worth is a key factor in the individual's continued participation, understanding of equality, and excellence in education. The likelihood that individuals will feel secure and have a high level of confidence among large groups of peers of different ethnic backgrounds and physical abilities is increased through the inclusion of deliberate student learning outcomes. This approach offers one specific multicultural outcome for each individual and partner activity.

In Step Two, the teacher introduces the activity and identifies the names of individuals that have greatly influenced others to participate in individual or dual sports. This brief information gives importance to the activity and fosters appreciation for the achievements of famous sport heroes from the past or accomplished contemporary athletes that can be admired and serve as role models. Feelings of self-worth grow when the individual is asked to assume one half of the responsibility in completing vigorous challenges or cooperative tasks involving a partner. To begin, the teacher adopts techniques that increase the likelihood of individuals working with different partners throughout the year. These techniques are identified on page 8. Following this teaching practice, the newly formed partners are now given the responsibility of measuring and preparing the playing area to include sport markings and boundaries that are often unlike those utilized in most gymnasiums in the USA, or they may perform other tasks like reviewing a creative worksheet so that it can be administered during a partner fitness activity. These small, yet purposeful, preparatory tasks are critical in helping partners feel at ease with one another and instill an eagerness to participate.

In Step Three, the teacher introduces the actual physical challenge for the two individuals to complete, and suggests a "peer practice component," described on page 12, that allows for sufficient trials to accommodate both individuals' varying physical skill levels. This teaching practice assists the student in valuing the contributions of a classmate, and helps the individual to consider a peer's different viewpoint. The teacher initiates the activity by having all partners exercise cooperative gestures before any competitive partner challenge, and is firm to discourage belittling comments and ethnic slang throughout the lesson. Statements such as these often occur within schools having large multicultural populations and class sizes, and perpetuate racial and cultural misunderstanding.

In Step Four, the teacher encourages individuals to share statements of self-reflection. This process is geared toward the student recognizing his or her importance in the learning process, and therefore increases the individual's feeling of self-worth. Self-assessment

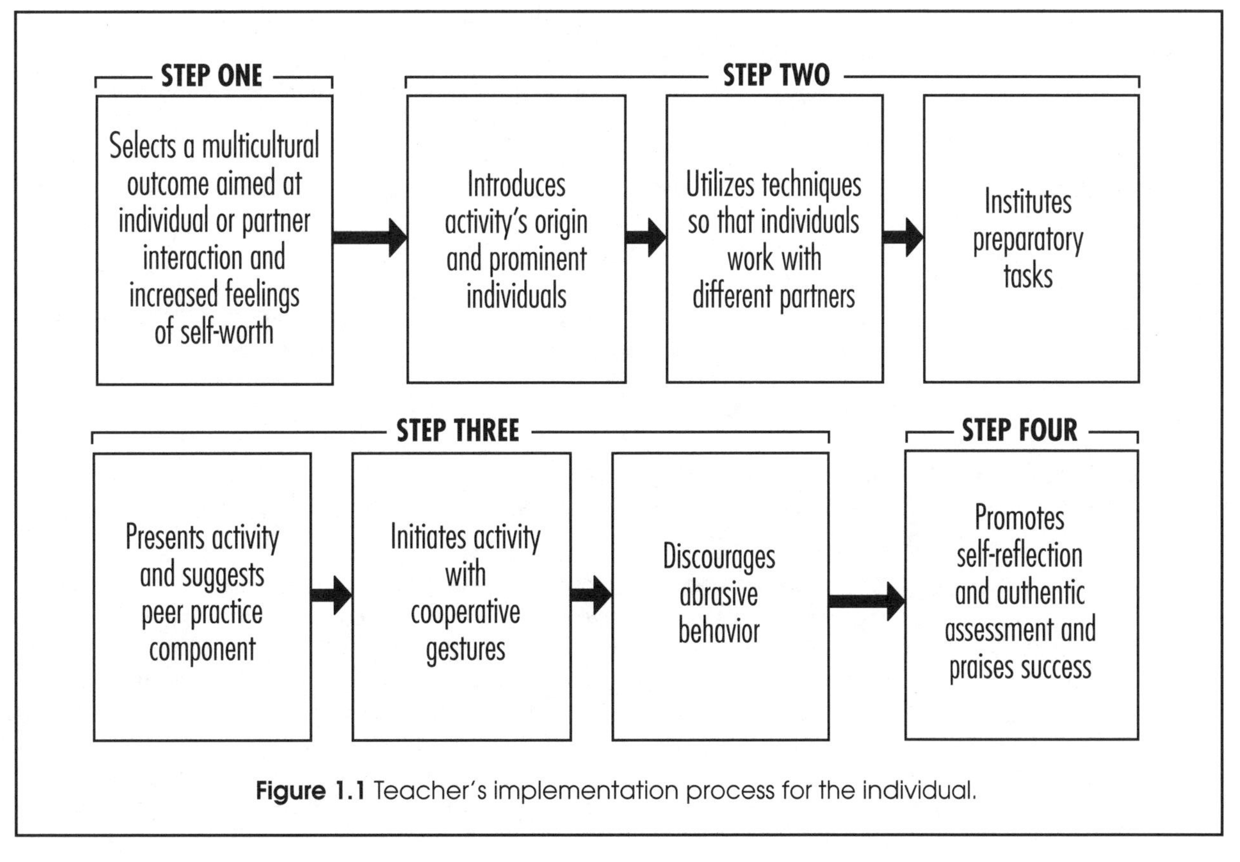

Figure 1.1 Teacher's implementation process for the individual.

is discussed on page 12. The teacher's implementation process for the individual is completed with the teacher making a conscious effort to acknowledge the sense of gratification that an individual feels after successfully participating with another classmate.

THE TEACHER'S IMPLEMENTATION PROCESS FOR THE GROUP

Not surprisingly, the teacher's implementation process for the group has similar characteristics to the teacher's implementation process for the individual. This was not always the case during the field-testing of the suggested group activities. In the fourth year of the field-testing, the practicing teachers strongly voiced a need for greater ease in the group implementation process. Likewise, written student comments indicated that many students found a new format difficult to follow and missed the process that they were accustomed to in earlier lessons involving partners. In addition, the authors were unaware of several complex variables that hampered group learning, such as limited English-speaking abilities and the confusion that can occur when introducing games and sports that are totally unfamiliar to the students. We discovered that it worked better to maintain many of the approach characteristics that were used in the process of implementing the individual and partner outcomes, and to revise or expand the approach only when it was apparent that group process necessitated change. Consequently, the teacher's implementation process for the group uses a similar format.

In Step One of the teacher's implementation process for the group, the teacher selects a multicultural outcome that is aimed at positive group interaction and fostering feelings of pride. Other outcomes that form the basis of multicultural education are culture, change, conflict resolution, pluralism, cooperation, empathy, and tolerance. The physical education setting provides many opportunities to convey these and similar outcomes so that all students can achieve success in a group situation.

In Step Two, the teacher's statement of purpose includes the origin and growth of a particular activity, as well as the groups of people that were most responsible for the activity's success. This information not only sparks the group's interest, but also increases the students' understanding of the cultures, identities, and histories of the diverse groups that comprise our society. Step Two also uses specific grouping practices that do not create racially, ethnically, or gender identifiable groups. Specific grouping strategies are identified on page 9 of the text. The step also increases the student's appreciation for either modified versions of sports common to the USA, or team sport activities frequently played by other cultures, as the teacher assigns groups of students to preparatory tasks similar to those found in Step One of the implementation process for the individual. These include being accountable for unusual floor or field markings and the construction of innovative sport equipment. This element piques the group's curiosity, and communicates the idea that the students will perform unique physical activity experiences in contrast to traditional sport content often described by today's adolescent as being "the same old, same old," and nurtures group commitment.

In Step Three, the teacher may demonstrate a complex skill, or have a trial demonstration of the game, to alleviate any confusion concerning the rules. Among other factors, the trial demonstration can also be used to reinforce the need to consider the health and welfare of the group during competitive physical activity, or to structure the game play so that the more skilled students within a group do not dominate the activity. This is possible by avoiding rules that refer to either sex (e.g., a girl must touch the ball at least once in order for the goal to count), and instead, gives the teacher the opportunity to identify a specific number of passes that must be made before shooting a goal, or the playing positions that must make contact with the ball before a goal is scored, to insure full participation.

Increased group interaction is also addressed in Step Three through the use of a physical education "forum," which is described on page 12 of this text. From a historical and international perspective, group forums have played a critical role in the development of rules and strategies. In this approach, game play is briefly stopped so that students can share ideas, express concerns, identify any negative aspects of various activities, and make modification to rules. Throughout the lesson, the teacher discourages slang and ethnic name calling, insists on cooperative gestures during competitive activity, and applauds group success.

In the final step of the approach, Step Four, the teacher promotes group discussion and uses one or more forms of authentic assessment techniques to appraise the group's shared sense of pride and accomplishment.

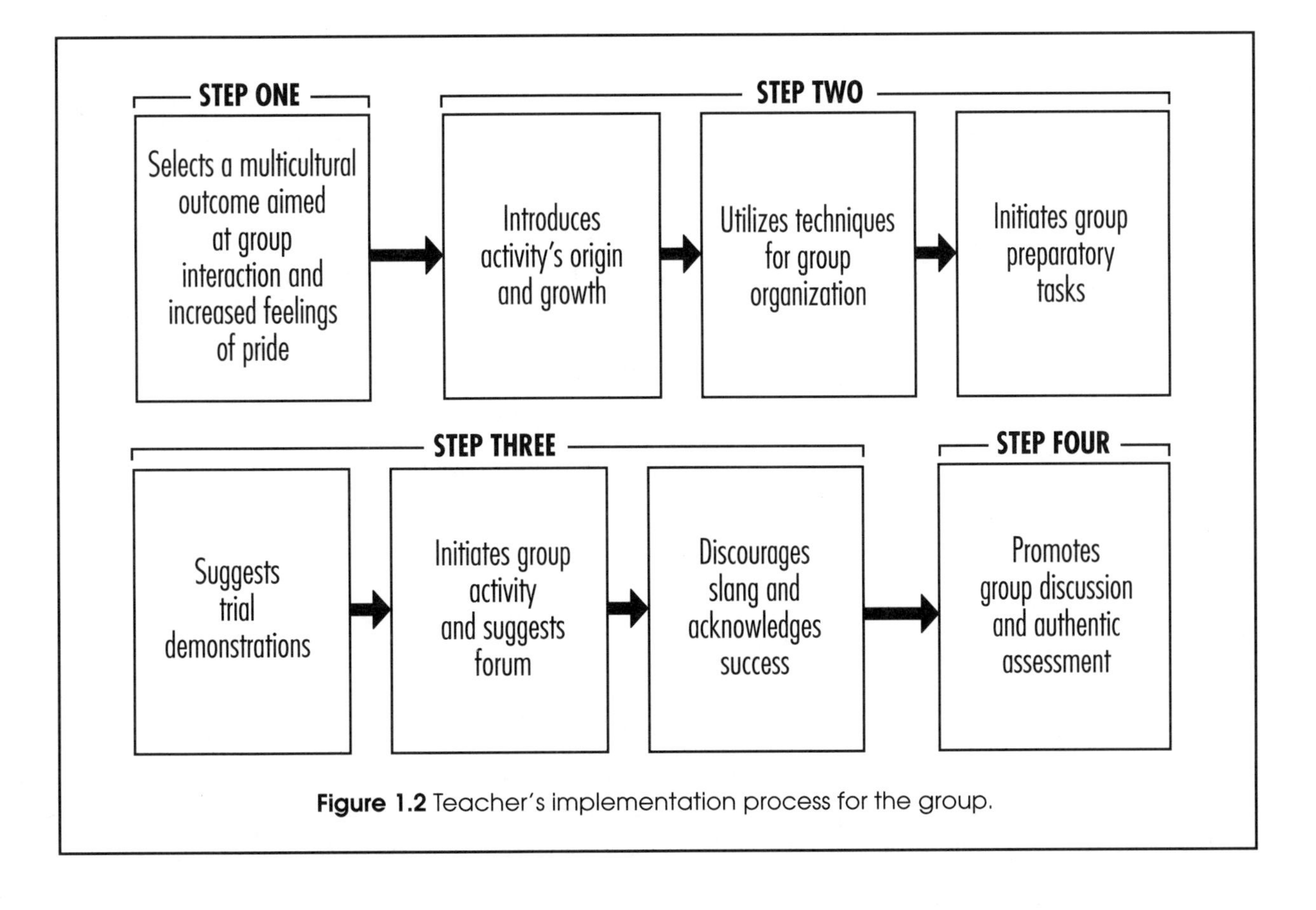

Figure 1.2 Teacher's implementation process for the group.

TEACHING PRACTICES THAT INCREASE PARTICIPATION

When utilizing this resource's multicultural approach, it is critical that the teacher exhibit behavior that extends beyond that used in executing class procedures. The following practices establish a plan of action that reflects the teacher's behavior for the purpose of increased student cooperation and participation.

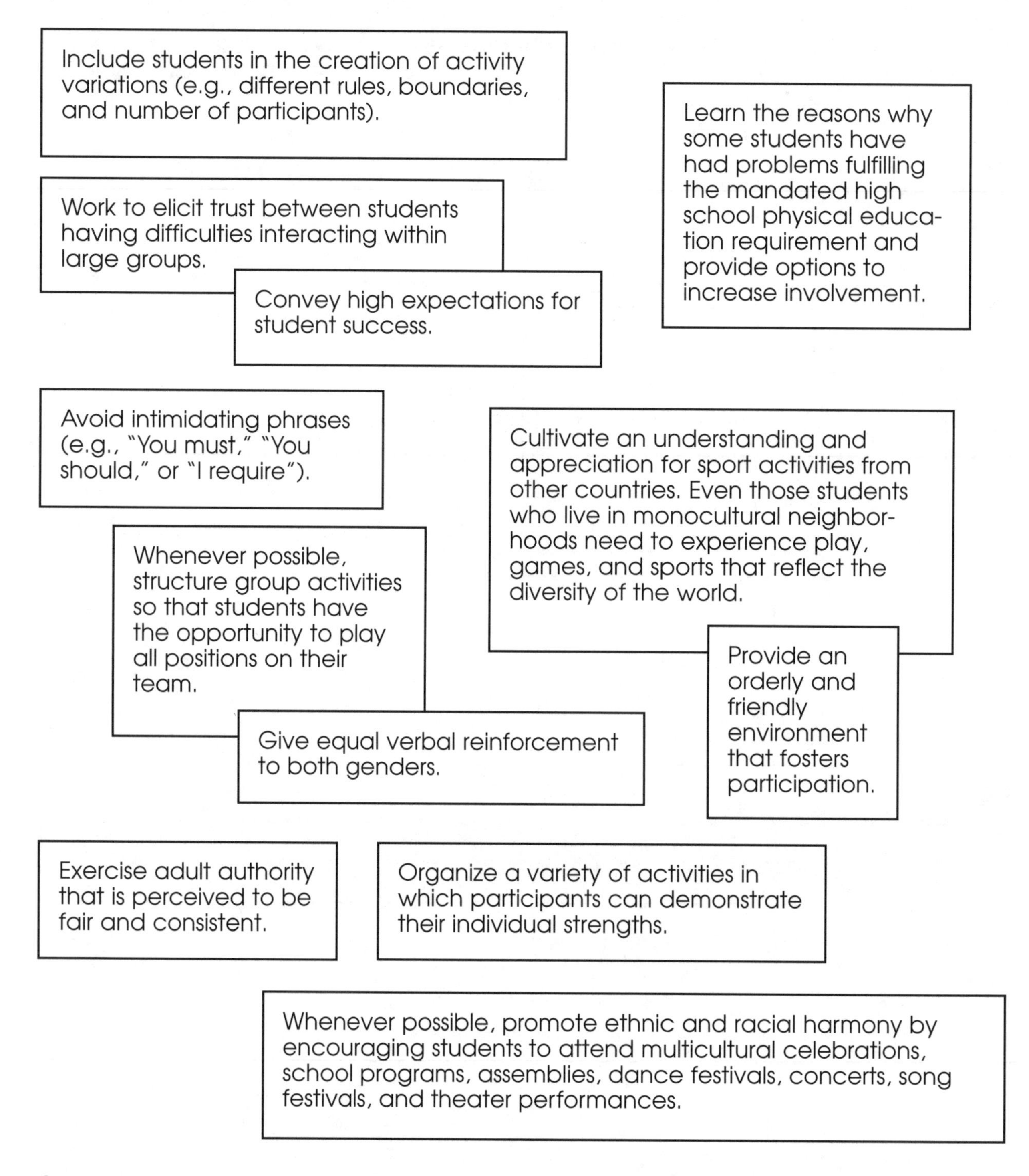

CHAPTER

2

The Use of a Simplified Lesson Format and Multicultural Outcomes

IDENTIFYING MULTICULTURAL OUTCOMES

In the simplest sense, the term *outcome* means result. Academically, an outcome refers to a change in the student's behavior due to participation in learning experiences. Outcomes are what teachers anticipate will materialize if students learn. The multicultural outcomes offered in this book represent a change in the student's behavior that ultimately lead to increased feelings of self-worth and group pride. For ease of implementation, they are presented as one word or phrase and therefore become the desired result at the end of the lesson.

Each activity is presented in a simplified lesson format that includes one multicultural outcome, a brief description of the activity to increase the student's cognitive awareness and appreciation of the activity, the necessary playing space, and the essential rules. The text also explains additional activities and techniques that can be implemented into the lesson format.

PREPARING THE BODY FOR PHYSICAL ACTIVITY

The time allocated for most warm-up sessions should be brief and dependent upon the intensity of the selected activity. Many of the lessons do not require an extended number of muscle stretches to prepare the student for participation. In these lessons (e.g., shufflecurl), the normal warm-up session should not exceed three to five minutes.

In lessons requiring more vigorous physical activity, it is recommended that students be given a choice in the selection of a particular stretch or exercise. This is possible by using open ended questions or suggestions in contrast to telling the student to perform a specific calisthenic. For example, the teacher might challenge the entire class by asking, "Can you perform an exercise while bending at your waist?" In this example, individuals might respond by touching their toes, by demonstrating a sit up, or by executing side stretches. Other example phrases or questions could include:

- Can you demonstrate an exercise that requires you to move your arms quickly?
- Show me an exercise done in a sitting position.
- Is it possible to keep your feet very still and exercise only your upper body?
- Let's see an exercise that requires you to use both arms and legs.
- Show me an exercise that involves twisting or turning.
- Create an exercise that stretches the biceps.
- Can you perform an exercise that makes your heart pump faster?

This choice element for daily stretches should help eliminate phrases such as, "Do we have to do sit ups?," "I hate jumping jacks," or "Toe touches again!", all of which have become routine in the warm-up segment of many daily lessons.

PARTNER SELECTION TECHNIQUES

Interpersonal relationships are more likely to occur when individuals are encouraged to work with different partners throughout the school year. The techniques listed in this section facilitate this process and help students to identify basic similarities and interests. Allow no more than 10 to 15 seconds, and repeat the techniques throughout the lesson so that students are not always working with the same individuals.

Individuals should be encouraged to work with a partner who has these features:

- The same shoe size, number of eyelets
- The same height
- The same arm extension
- The same birth month
- The same first initial
- The same last initial
- The same number of vowels in their first name
- The same number of vowels in their last name
- The same number of letters in their first name
- The same number of letters in their last name
- The same number of brothers
- The same number of sisters
- The same favorite rock and roll group
- The same favorite basketball, baseball, or football team
- The same favorite novel
- The same favorite school subject
- The same favorite hobby

GROUP SELECTION TECHNIQUES

Teachers should avoid choosing captains who are responsible for dividing their peers into teams. Disagreements can occur, in addition to lowering the self-image of those chosen last. One alternative to this technique involves asking the students to make a side-by-side line. On the teacher's signal, have the students close their eyes and respond to one of the following actions:

- Either jump one step forward or one step backward.
- Either stretch the body upwardly, or stoop downward.
- Either make a grip with the right hand or with the left hand.
- Either make an X with your arms in front of the body or make an O with your arms stretched above the head.
- Pretend to catch a ground ball or a fly ball.

Teachers can also cut small strips of construction paper and have the students pull a colored strip from a hat or envelope. Or students can be asked to write a number on a small piece of paper, and the teacher can divide the group according to odd or even numbers. Or students can be divided according to those having birthdays in the month of January through June or July through December. In all cases, alternative grouping techniques increase the likelihood that students will experience a more friendly form of competition, and will participate in different groups throughout the year.

The Chinese Method Of Selecting Groups

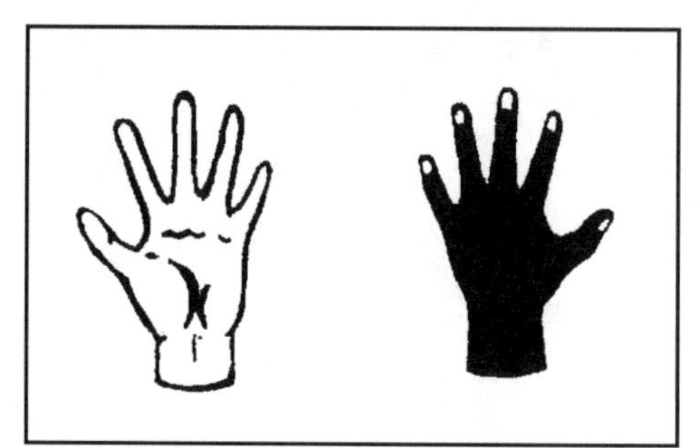

The Chinese people have a unique technique to select teams. To begin, all students stand in a circle with their hands flat on their chests. On the teacher's count of three, each student puts one hand into the circle either palm up or palm down. Palm up is called white and palm down represents black. In the event that the outcome is not even, the teacher asks the players from the largest group to repeat the action until the teams are equal in number. If the result ends with one person representing the odd number, that player steps away from the students who are choosing. After the class has two teams, the player returns and either says black or white, without knowing who is on which team, thereby teams are selected totally according to chance.

The Roman Method Of Selecting Groups

Many Italian coaches and physical education teachers divide their groups into two teams by first asking all students to form one long line of players facing forward (figure 2.1 A). The teacher or coach walks down to the middle of the line and uses his or her hand to "slice" the line (B). The first player (where the slice occurred) walks or "marches" up to the front, followed by all remaining players (C). The group is now two equal teams (D).

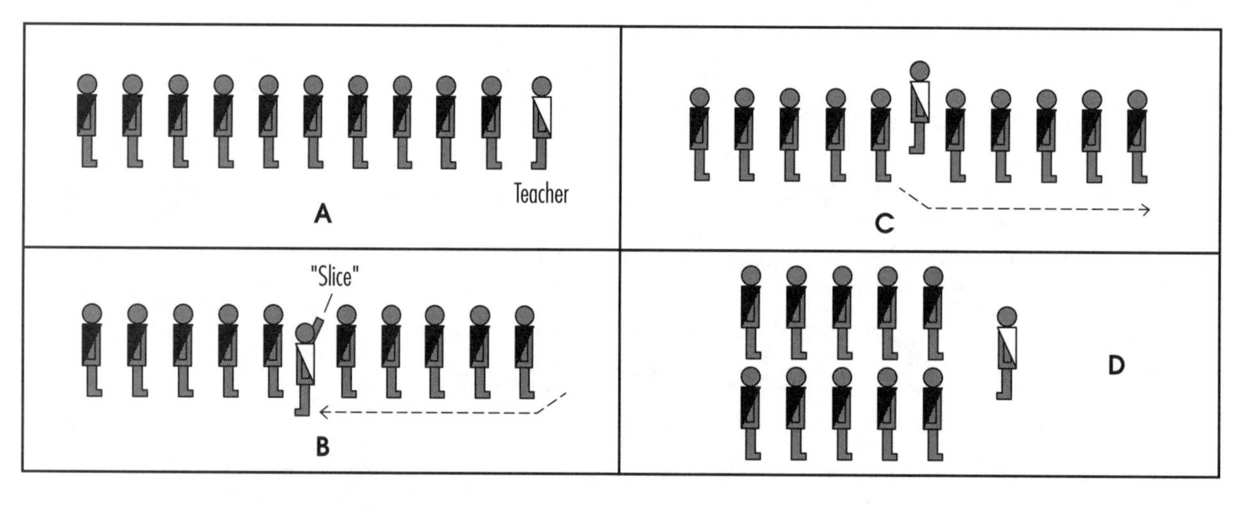

Figure 2.1 The Roman group selection method.

The Brazilian Method Of Selecting Groups

Many Brazilian coaches and physical activity teachers use a very quick and effective technique to divide a large group into two teams. To begin, the teacher asks all players to form a long line with each player standing behind another (figure 2.2, frame 1). The teacher stands at the front of the line and begins to "walk into" the line of players while also using one hand to signal which side a student should quickly step to so that the teacher can pass (2). Upon the teacher's completion, the line of players have been divided into two groups (3).

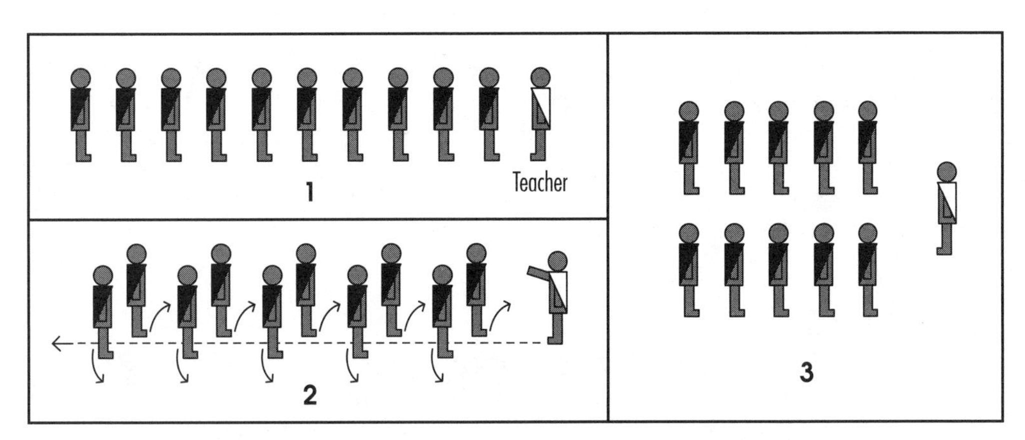

Figure 2.2 The Brazilian group selection method.

PRESENTATION OF THE SKILL, CONCEPT, OR ACTIVITY

When introducing a skill, concept, or activity, the teacher is encouraged to:

(a) Implement this resource's multicultural approach;

(b) Eliminate hazards to assist in the prevention of injuries;

(c) Reinforce the multicultural outcome of the lesson (e.g., "The purpose of today's activity is to...");

(d) Make the presentations as concise as possible by briefly using the information in each lesson's description of play;

(e) Distribute the equipment only after the introduction;

(f) Ask the individual, "What color stick would you like?" or "What position would you like to play?" Avoid asking the student if he or she wants to play;

(g) Encourage participation in a friendly manner ("Let's see," "Try this equipment," and "This looks as though it is fun"), or use photographs to assist the student's understanding; and

(h) Use vocabulary words that are in the student's current repertoire.

STUDENT INVOLVEMENT

Many of the activities for increased individual interaction ask partners to prepare or create the learning experience. This is possible when the students use rulers, yard sticks, or measuring tape. Three-foot strips of string can be cut in advance so that large classes will have ample measurement devices. The following facts can be conveyed to the students to spark their participation:

A foot is the average length of an adult foot. In ancient times it equalled 11.5 inches, but today it is always 12 inches (30 cm).

A yard equals 3 feet or 91 centimeters. This was the average length of a man's belt in ancient times.

The Roman mile, pronounced *mille,* was based on 1,000 paces of a marching army and was much shorter than today's mile, which measures 5,280 feet. A pace was equal to two steps (about 5 feet), unlike today's one step forward.

All students are encouraged to participate throughout the lesson or during some part of it. Individuals should not be forced to participate since this action most often results in a confrontation between the student and the teacher. Play should begin without the individual. At some point in the activity, the teacher should ask a student who has demonstrated enthusiasm to approach this reluctant individual and suggest that he or she change roles, thereby allowing a natural form of substitution. In most cases, peer reinforcement is successful.

PEER PRACTICE COMPONENT

Each class should be allotted a specified practice period, referred to as *peer practice,* in which individuals work with their classmates to improve their skill performance. This critical element also encourages individual and partner cooperation and learning.

ESSENTIAL RULES FOR PLAY

Rules should be implemented while the game is in progress. Whenever possible, the activity should be introduced as having similar rules or strategies of a well-known sport (e.g., "Ring hockey uses many of the same strategies as ice hockey or field hockey"). This facilitates the learning process.

THE FORUM

The forum is a critical feature of the multicultural approach for group interaction. Teachers should allocate a specific period of time (5 to 7 minutes) for an informal forum. The forum should be used for discussions related to rules, participation, or issues reflecting student or teacher concerns. The forum encourages each student to have a voice in his or her learning process, and promotes group cooperation.

ASSESSMENT

Reflect upon the lesson's outcome. Ask yourself if students' displayed behavior coincided with the outcome. If not, ask yourself what changes could be made for greater success in the future, and use the sample rubrics found on pages 147-149.

PART II
GAMES AND ACTIVITIES

CHAPTER
3

Activities for Increased Individual Interaction

PARTNER STUNTS AND STRETCHES

Greece

OUTCOME

Demonstrate partner cooperation

DESCRIPTION OF PLAY

The ancient Greeks are credited with instituting the value and joy of exercise. They believed that a healthy body and a healthy mind created the whole person. However, it was not until the early 1950s when Jeremy N. Morris, a British physician, developed what has become known as *exercise hypnosis* that focused on exercising to decrease the risk for coronary artery disease, that the exercise revolution of the 1970s spread worldwide. In this activity, the student cooperates with a partner to perform a variety of creative stunts and stretches emphasizing flexibility, balance, and strength.

PLAYING SPACE

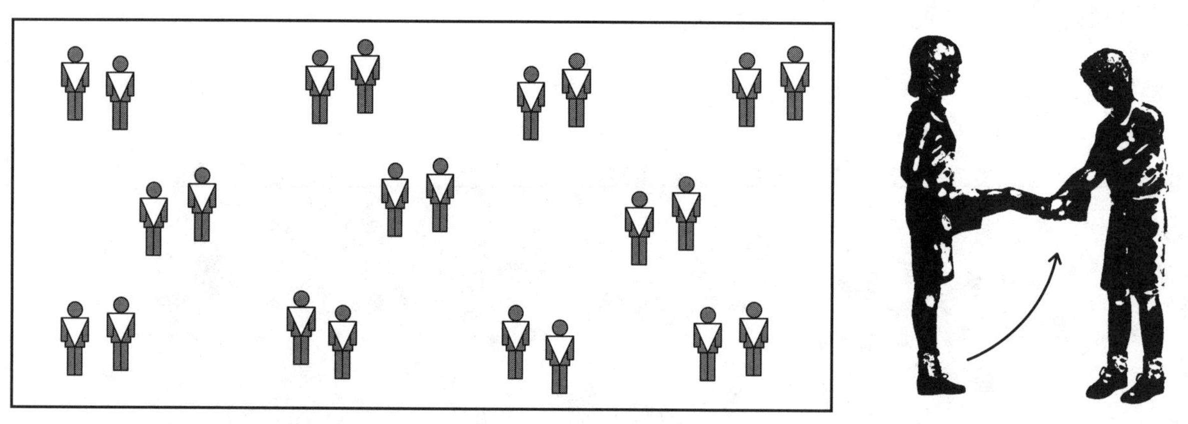

EQUIPMENT

Gymnastic mats are recommended, but not required

ESSENTIAL RULES FOR PLAY

1. Duplicate the stunts & stretches cards on pages 15 and 16. Partners select one stunt or exercise card from the stack of cards. The cards should be positioned face down.
2. The two students read the card's instruction and perform the activity.
3. Following a 3- to 5-minute peer practice session, each set of partners announces the name of their activity, explains the actions, and demonstrates the stunt or exercise to classmates.
4. All students are challenged to perform the stunt or exercise following the partner demonstration.
5. Play continues as each set of partners demonstrates a stunt to the class.
6. Self-Reflection Question - Did I assist my partner's efforts to help guarantee success?

TRICKY TRIANGLE STRETCH

a. Students stand approximately 4 feet in front of their partners and extend their arms forward (palm to palm).

b. While leaning forward, both individuals slowly step backward approximately three steps.

c. Partners stay in this position for 5 seconds.

ON THE UP AND UP PUSHUP

Partner Stunts and Stretches

a. One student lies on his or her back with the knees bent and feet placed flat on the floor. This student grasps the ankles of the partner, who has assumed a pushup position.

b. The student performing the pushup is at a low level (4-6 inches) to the floor.

c. The student lying on his or her back straightens the arms and lifts the feet as high as possible.

d. The partner in the pushup position also straightens his or her arms and holds the position for 5 seconds.

e. Exchange roles.

WITH A LITTLE HELP FROM A FRIEND

Partner Stunts and Stretches

a. One student extends his or her arms upward, directly behind the back. Both feet are flat on the floor.

b. The second student stands behind the first and grasps the arms in order that the first student can stretch forward.

c. Stay in this position for 5 seconds.

d. Exchange roles.

TOWERS

Partner Stunts and Stretches

a. Both students assume the pushup position, with arms bent and the chest close to the floor.

b. One partner places his or her shins on the second partner's back.

c. Both students push the body upward in a pushup position for 5 seconds.

d. Exchange roles.

BRIDGE WORK

a. One student makes a box shape with his or her body by kneeling and placing the palms on the floor, with the arms perpendicular.

b. The second student places his or her ankles on the student's back, and uses the arms and hands for support to keep the body's weight off the floor.

c. Partners should maintain this position for 5 seconds and exchange roles.

Partner Stunts and Stretches

BE BACK IN A MINUTE

a. Students stand back to back with their partners.

b. One partner lifts his or her arms straight overhead and leans backward. The other bends at the knees and grasps the partner's wrists.

c. This same partner leans forward and lifts the partner slightly off the floor, supporting the other's weight. Partners maintain this position for 5 seconds.

Partner Stunts and Stretches

TOGETHER WE CAN

a. Students stand facing each other with hands placed on each other's shoulders.

b. Both students raise the left leg backward as high as possible without arching the back.

c. Partners should hold this position for 5 seconds.

Partner Stunts and Stretches

STUDENT-DEVELOPED MOVEMENT ROUTINES

France

OUTCOME

Exhibit creativity

DESCRIPTION OF PLAY

Olga Korbut, a world renowned gymnast, was born in 1955 in Grodno, Soviet Union. Her physical education teacher believed she had the potential to become a gymnast. In 1972, after her sixth consecutive gold medal, ABC's Wide World of Sports selected her as their Athlete of the Year. In this French activity, partners develop a movement routine by linking six distinctive balances, holds, and jumps.

PLAYING SPACE

EQUIPMENT

Dynamic music and a tape player, two to three gymnastic mats if available

ESSENTIAL RULES FOR PLAY

1. Duplicate the movement cards on pages 18 – 20, so that partners can select six different movement cards.
2. The students arrange the cards in a logical progression with the goal of creating a movement sequence. Partners conduct a peer practice session to link the movements together until a natural flow between movements is obvious.
3. The students have the option of one partner demonstrating the routine followed by his or her partner's demonstration, or one student may perform a movement followed by the partner's performance of the second movement.
4. Whenever possible, gymnastic mats should be incorporated into the lesson for individuals desiring to add tumbling skills to their sequence of six movements. Individuals should be encouraged to ask their partners for assistance in spotting advanced balances when necessary.
5. Whenever possible, incorporate dynamic music to stimulate student participation.
6. Extension - Depending on the availability of mats, several cards can be marked with a star to represent a compulsory exercise. The students can be instructed to select one to three compulsory exercises depending on their capabilities.
7. Self-Reflection Question - Did I move easily between the balances, holds, and jumps?

POSITION 1
Student-Developed Movement Routines
POSITION 2
Student-Developed Movement Routines
POSITION 3
Student-Developed Movement Routines
POSITION 4
Student-Developed Movement Routines
POSITION 5
Student-Developed Movement Routines
POSITION 6
Student-Developed Movement Routines
POSITION 7
Student-Developed Movement Routines
POSITION 8
Student-Developed Movement Routines

POSITION 9
Student-Developed Movement Routines
POSITION 10
Student-Developed Movement Routines
POSITION 11
Student-Developed Movement Routines
POSITION 12
Student-Developed Movement Routines
POSITION 13
Student-Developed Movement Routines
POSITION 14
Student-Developed Movement Routines
POSITION 15
Student-Developed Movement Routines
POSITION 16
Student-Developed Movement Routines

POSITION 17
Student-Developed Movement Routines
POSITION 18
Student-Developed Movement Routines
POSITION 19
Student-Developed Movement Routines
POSITION 20
Student-Developed Movement Routines
POSITION 21
Student-Developed Movement Routines
POSITION 22
Student-Developed Movement Routines
POSITION 23
Student-Developed Movement Routines
Wild Card
Student's Choice of Movement or Stance
POSITION 24
Student-Developed Movement Routines

RIBBON BALL ROUTINES

China

OUTCOME

Communicate rhythmically

DESCRIPTION OF PLAY

Based on an ancient Chinese Ribbon Dance, today's commercially manufactured ribbon ball consists of a 13- to 15-foot colorful vinyl or plastic ribbon attached to a small rubber ball. Most manufactured models include an elastic string for gripping. With the addition of music, partners are challenged to demonstrate a variety of rhythmical movements.

PLAYING SPACE

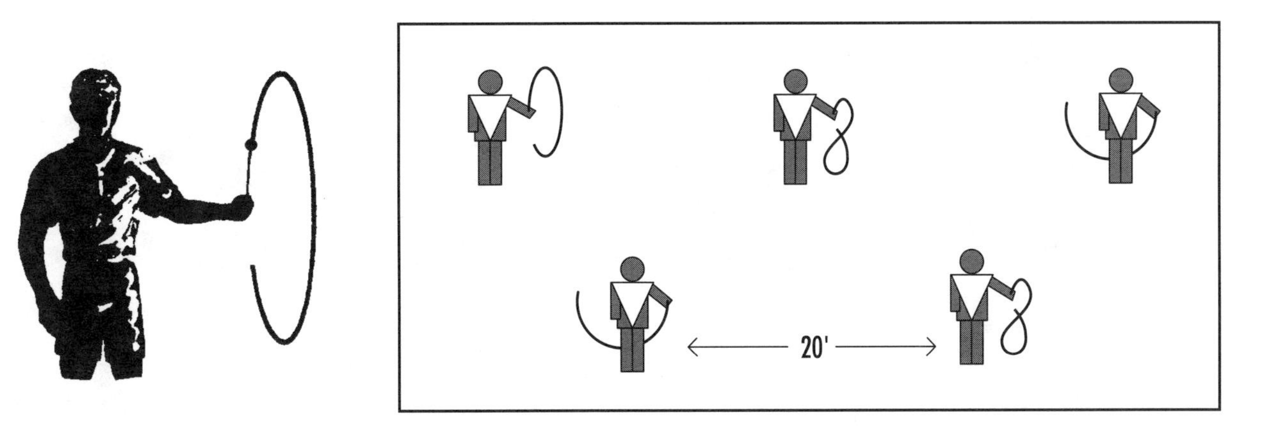

EQUIPMENT

Dynamic music, tape player, ribbon balls or strips of ribbon. When commercially manufactured ribbon balls are not available, a roll of decorator or 1-inch gift-wrapping ribbon can be cut into 5-foot strips and used as a substitute.

ESSENTIAL RULES FOR PLAY

1. No student should stand closer than 20 feet in any direction from a classmate when using a ribbon ball.
2. Ribbon balls should not be thrown or bounced in limited spaces.
3. Partners are challenged to develop their own ribbon ball routine, consisting of four or more of the suggested patterns during a peer practice session.
4. Individuals are encouraged to keep a natural flow of movement for a period of 2 minutes, and to duplicate their partner's patterns.
5. Play lively music.
6. Self-Reflection Question - Did I swing the ball to the beat of the music and demonstrate my partner's suggested movement patterns?

TYPICAL PATTERNS OF MOVEMENT

Front circles

Side circles

Above the head circles

The swing

The tornado

Figure eight

Art initials

Spell a word

Student creations

AEROBIC RAP

OUTCOME

Generate self-expression

DESCRIPTION OF PLAY

Aerobic dancing is a physical fitness program that became popular in the middle 1970s. Jacki Sorensen was one of the first fitness experts to choreograph routines aimed at toning muscle, burning calories, and improving relaxation and cardiovascular fitness. In this activity, students are encouraged to bring in compact discs or tapes of their favorite Rap or other popular music and work with a partner to develop a 60-second aerobic movement routine. A variation of movements is encouraged.

PLAYING SPACE

EQUIPMENT

Dynamic music and tape player or compact disc player

ESSENTIAL RULES FOR PLAY

1. Partners develop an aerobic rap routine based on a combination of three or more movements that can be written on a large poster for all students to view.
2. *Stretching and Clapping* - Students reach with the arms up and clap while bending at the knees to the beat of the music.
3. *Knee Ups* - Students bend the right or left knee while bringing it up to the chest. *Variation* - Students raise a knee upward and clap hands underneath the leg.
4. *Stretch to the Side* - With one or both arms in the air, students stretch overhead to the right side and then the left.
5. *Kicks* - Alternate kicks to the right, left, front, and back.
6. *Heel Lifts* - Standing with the legs parallel and slightly separated, students lift their right heel, pressing high on the ball of the foot. Repeat with left heel.

7. Finger snaps, Three runs and a hop, Struts, Skips, Arms to the side, Torso circles, Lunges, and Leg swings out to the side are also encouraged.
8. With each action, partners should be encouraged to bend at the knees.
9. Individual expression is encouraged during the peer practice session. At some point, all partners perform their rap routines, without stopping, for 1 minute.
10. Self-Reflection Question - Did my routine include at least three different movements, and did I use a positive facial expression while performing?

HOLE IN ONE SOCCER

OUTCOME

Concentrate on a goal

DESCRIPTION OF PLAY

Soldiers in ancient China played *tsu-ch'iu* as part of their training using the head of their enemy as the ball. The early English players often used the gates of churches as their goals. Early soccer balls consisted of an inflated pig's bladder encased within tanned leather. They were not waterproof and required the player to use rawhide laces to stitch the last panel on the ball. The world famous player, Pele, was born in Tres Coracoes, Brazil. During his career with Brazil he scored more than 1,000 goals, and later played with the New York Cosmos. In this activity, the student is challenged to use the least number of soccer kicks to make contact with designated objects such as trees, buildings, signs, or plastic markers.

PLAYING SPACE

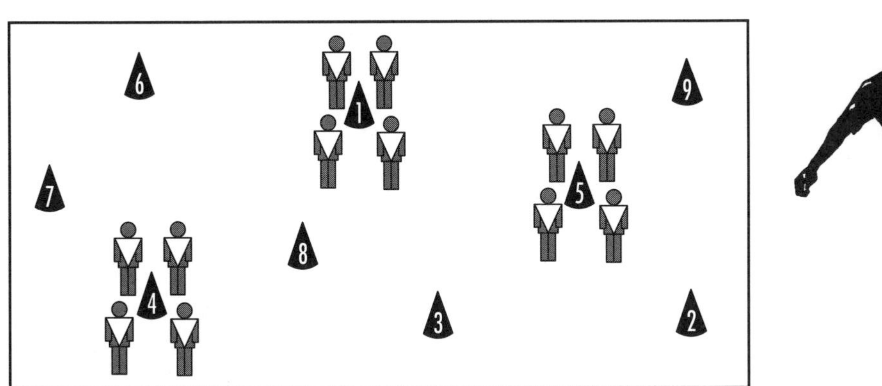

EQUIPMENT

Soccer balls for partners or groups of four players, markers, and cones

ESSENTIAL RULES FOR PLAY

1. The students identify nine or eighteen objects in the environment to represent golf holes. Each object is identified with a number or a marker.
2. Partners conduct a peer practice session focusing on the instep soccer kick to increase the likelihood of accuracy and success.
3. Each set of partners space themselves at different numbered holes. One player places a soccer ball on a designated tee area and kicks the ball toward the fairway.
4. Players take turns and continue to kick the ball toward the hole, through and around obstacles, until the ball touches the designated target (e.g., fence post) or a gymnasium cone.
5. The total number of kicks per hole can be recorded on a score sheet.

6. The total score is calculated for a 9- or 18-hole course.
7. Extension - Two sets of partners cooperate to play "best ball." Each individual team member tees off. The ball that lands closest to the hole is designated as the team ball for that hole. Team members continue to take a turn with the team's designated ball until contact is made with the hole. Only one score for the team is recorded.
8. Extension - Partners can perform the same activity while using flying discs.

9. Self-Reflection Question - Did I take the time to aim properly before kicking the ball?

SCORE				
HOLE	A	B	C	D
1				
2				
3				
4				
5				
6				
7				
8				
9				
TOTAL 1-9				
Have a good game				

SCORE				
HOLE	A	B	C	D
10				
11				
12				
13				
14				
15				
16				
17				
18				
TOTAL 10-18				
TOTAL 1-18				

SCORE				
HOLE	A	B	C	D
1				
2				
3				
4				
5				
6				
7				
8				
9				
TOTAL 1-9				
Have a good game				

SCORE				
HOLE	A	B	C	D
10				
11				
12				
13				
14				
15				
16				
17				
18				
TOTAL 10-18				
TOTAL 1-18				

SCORE				
HOLE	A	B	C	D
1				
2				
3				
4				
5				
6				
7				
8				
9				
TOTAL 1-9				
Have a good game				

SCORE				
HOLE	A	B	C	D
10				
11				
12				
13				
14				
15				
16				
17				
18				
TOTAL 10-18				
TOTAL 1-18				

SCORE				
HOLE	A	B	C	D
1				
2				
3				
4				
5				
6				
7				
8				
9				
TOTAL 1-9				
Have a good game				

SCORE				
HOLE	A	B	C	D
10				
11				
12				
13				
14				
15				
16				
17				
18				
TOTAL 10-18				
TOTAL 1-18				

SUPER SHOTS

OUTCOME

Participate fully in cooperative endeavors

DESCRIPTION OF PLAY

Basketball was created by James A. Naismith in 1891 in Springfield, Massachusetts, where he secured two wooden peach baskets to a gymnasium balcony to serve as targets for a thrown soccer ball. A ladder was used to remove the ball from the basket. In Super Shots individuals or partners record the number of set shots needed to score a basket from different designated floor markings.

PLAYING SPACE

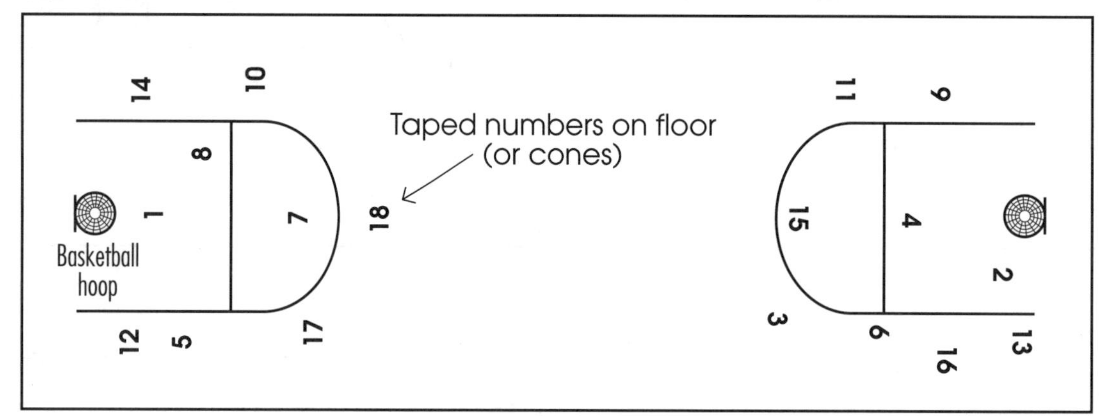

EQUIPMENT

Masking tape, basketballs, score sheets, and a minimum of two basketball hoops

ESSENTIAL RULES FOR PLAY

1. Conduct a peer practice session to review the techniques of the one- or two-hand set shot.
2. Distribute Super Shots score sheets to all students. Partners may begin shooting from any taped or chalked number on the playing floor.
3. Partners alternate shooting from the same designated spot until the shot is successful.
4. Partners record the number of shots that were taken to score a basket.
5. Each set of partners must finish one complete game at a time (e.g., numbers 1-18 in Trial One) before moving on to Trial Two or Three.
6. Extension - Partners receive only two shots from each spot. If one shot goes in the basket, they receive the point value of that spot. If both shots are successful, they receive double the point spot.
7. Self-Reflection Question - Was there less pressure to score when working with a partner?

SUPER SHOTS SCORE SHEET

NAME(S) ______________________________

INSTRUCTIONS

Record the number of shots needed to sink a basket for each floor marking. For example, if it takes three shots before a ball goes through the basket at spot 7, you place a 3 next to hole 7. Your goal is to have the lowest score possible.

TRIAL ONE		TRIAL TWO		TRIAL THREE	
HOLE		HOLE		HOLE	
1		1		1	
2		2		2	
3		3		3	
4		4		4	
5		5		5	
6		6		6	
7		7		7	
8		8		8	
9		9		9	
10		10		10	
11		11		11	
12		12		12	
13		13		13	
14		14		14	
15		15		15	
16		16		16	
17		17		17	
18		18		18	
TOTAL SCORE		TOTAL SCORE		TOTAL SCORE	

Grade 7-9 Complete numbers 1-8
Grade 10 Complete numbers 1-10
Grade 11 Complete numbers 1-14
Seniors Complete all 18 spots

Complete Trial One for all shots before moving on to Trial Two.

ACE, KING, QUEEN, OR JACK

Ireland

OUTCOME

Accept defeat gracefully

DESCRIPTION OF PLAY

Modern court handball rules originated in Ireland in 1884. Phil Casey, an Irish immigrant, built the first American handball court in Brooklyn, New York. Ace, King, Queen, or Jack is an adaptation of the earlier game. Two sets of partners stand in front of a wall that has been divided into four sections. Students identify themselves as either "ace," "king," "queen," or "jack." A small rubber ball is dropped and served (handball style) into one of the four sections. The student whose wall section was involved must respond and return the ball after one bounce into a different court section.

PLAYING SPACE

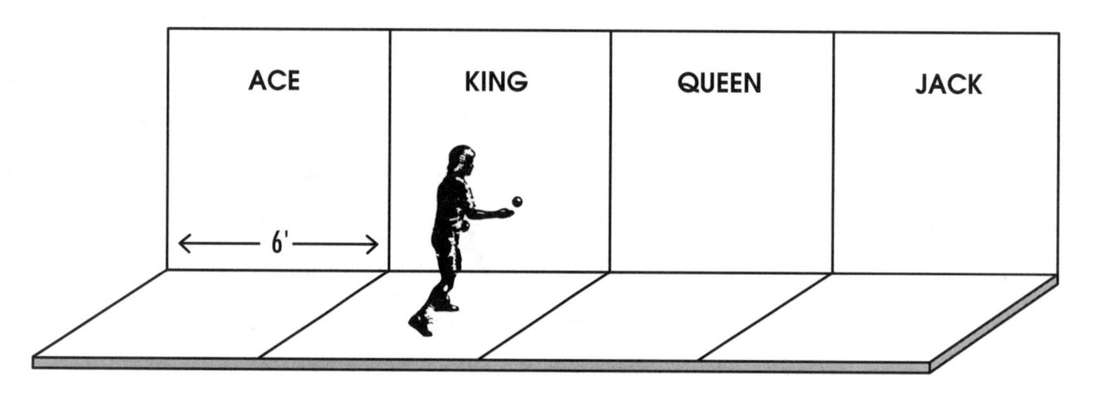

EQUIPMENT

Several rolls of masking tape and one 6- to 8-inch playground ball for every four to eight players. A tennis ball can also be used, although greater skill is required.

ESSENTIAL RULES FOR PLAY

1. Individuals within the class use masking tape to construct as many playing courts as space allows. Each court consists of four taped wall areas that are approximately 6 feet wide. Students stand 5 to 6 feet (or one body length) from the wall. The wall is referred to as the *court.*
2. Partners conduct a peer practice session to increase their abilities to serve and hit a small rubber ball off the wall for either a predetermined number of consecutive hits, or until individuals are at ease with the primary skill. Two sets of partners enter a court and exchange hand shakes with all players before game play.
3. Service begins with the "Ace" player. The serve must start with a bounce to the ground before the ball hits the wall, and be followed by an underhand cupped-slap of the ball off the wall into the "King's" court section. That player then uses the same techniques to hit it into the "Queen's" box and so on. When the last player

receives the ball, he or she switches the ball's direction hitting it back on its journey toward the Ace box.

4. The serve may not rebound off the wall lower than 3 feet from the floor or ground.
5. Each time a person fails to return the ball or serves incorrectly, he or she is awarded a "strike," and moves to the end of the court. Five strikes against a student removes him or her from the court. The "Ace" continues to serve until he or she is awarded one strike, at which point the "King" begins to serve. Play continues until one student remains or "rules the court." All students re-enter the court at this time and initiate a new game, or if necessary, four new students use the court so that all students within the class can have a turn.
6. The game is also called "Ace, King, and Queen" in some metropolitan cities in the USA.
7. Depending on the initial success, individuals may substitute the playground ball with a smaller ball more common to handball.
8. Extension - Individuals drop serve and kick the ball in one of the four sections. Individuals respond by kicking the ball back into one of the four sections. This extension requires individuals standing further from the wall, although the level of difficulty is approximately the same as the original version.
9. Self-Reflection Question - Did I display sportsmanship when I was eliminated from the court?

DO YOU DARE FOUR SQUARE

England

OUTCOME

Utilize self-control

DESCRIPTION OF PLAY

The English play numerous games involving boxes or squares painted on the ground. The game of Four Square is common to schools and recreational settings worldwide. Lines scratched into the dirt or painted on asphalt surfaces replaced the need for one- and four-well courts, which are commonly used in handball. In this activity, one student serves a 6- to 10-inch playground ball into an opponent's box. The student receiving the ball must return the serve into one of three box playing areas. Action continues until the ball is not properly returned into a box.

PLAYING SPACE

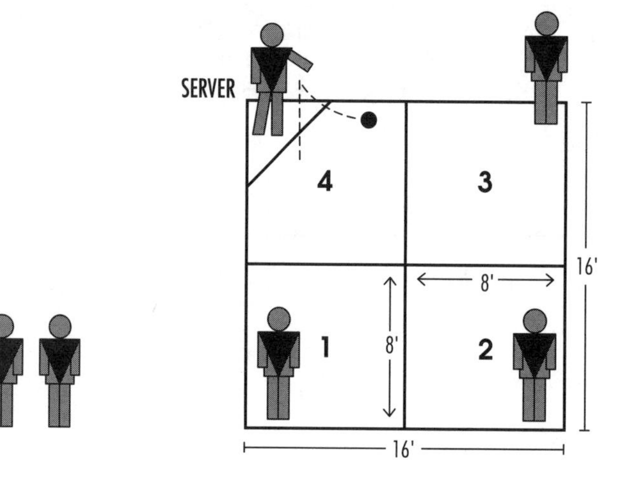

EQUIPMENT

Shoe polish or masking tape to create squares and one rubber playground ball for each square

ESSENTIAL RULES FOR PLAY

1. Students conduct a peer practice session by hitting a playground ball back and forth, underhand, with open palms.
2. Four students position themselves at the outside corner of each playing box. The student in the number 4 box is the server, and begins the action by saying, "Ready." The server then drops the ball into his or her own box and after the ball bounces once, it is tapped (underhand with open palms) into either box 1, 2, or 3.
3. Students respond to the serve by returning the ball with an underhand tap so that it falls into another student's box. The ball may not be caught or held, but should be returned with one or two open palms.
4. Action continues until a student fails to return the ball into a box. When a student is not able to return the serve, he or she moves to the end of the waiting line. With the exception of the server, all other students move to the next numbered box.

5. The objective is to remain or become the server in box 4.
6. Balls falling on the lines should be played. Overhand smashes are not permitted.
7. No ball can be returned by striking the ball with a closed fist.
8. Self-Reflection Question - Did I control my disappointment or anger when I failed to return a ball?
9. Extension - The server calls out, "Ready," followed by the words, "Around the Horn." The serve must be placed to the server's right or left and be hit consecutively from box to box until it returns to the server. This action continues until the server regains the ball or calls out a different variation.
10. Extension - The server calls out, "Ready," followed by the word, "Challenge." The server may serve to any student, but the ball must be returned to the server, until the server calls out, "End of challenge."
11. Extension - The server calls out, "Ready," followed by the word, "Duel." The serve can be placed to any one of the three players. The student receiving the serve must hit the ball back to the server, and the action continues between the two players until the server says, "End of duel."
12. Use a variety of different size balls to vary the degree of challenge. Basketballs, volleyballs, and even tennis balls require a very different degree of skill for success.

AROUND THE HORN

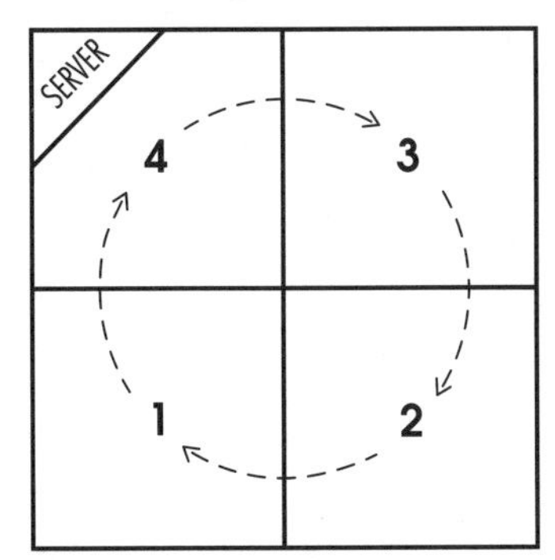

CHALLENGE

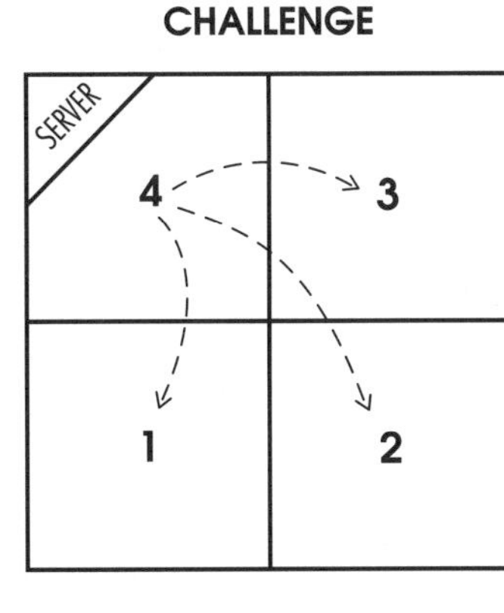

DUEL

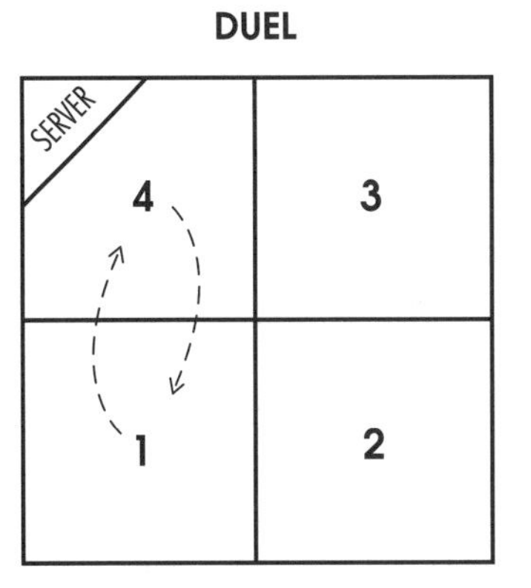

13. The word for ball in French is *balle,* and the Italian word for ball is *palla.*

CLOCK GOLF

Scotland

OUTCOME

Show consideration while waiting one's turn

DESCRIPTION OF PLAY

It is generally recognized that golf had early beginnings in Scotland, where shepherds hit round stones with long knotted sticks. The Scottish word *goulf* means to strike, and *divot* refers to a piece of turf. Mary, Queen of Scots, was said to be the first woman to play the game. In Clock Golf, students use a putting stroke common to golf, and strive to complete the 12-hole course in the least number of attempts.

PLAYING SPACE

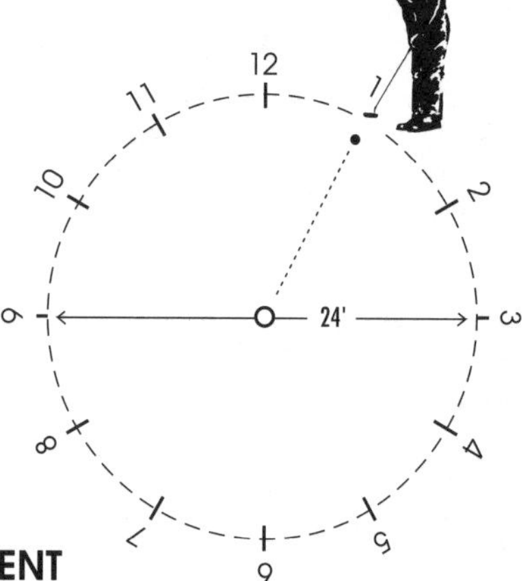

TOP GOLF TOURNAMENTS PLAYED WORLDWIDE

- British Open • U.S. Open
- U.S. PGA • U.S. Masters
- Ryder Cup – Male
- Curtis Cup – Female

EQUIPMENT

Putting irons, golf balls, and tin markers

ESSENTIAL RULES FOR PLAY

1. The students are responsible for designing the clock golf course. Place 12 markers equal distance from each other. Number each hole in the same manner as a clock. Place a tin container in the middle of the circle. Students can also create a 12-hole golf sheet.
2. Students conduct a peer practice session and observe each other's putting grip for accuracy. The ball must be struck with the putter's head, never pushed.
3. Students start from the tee located within the circle and attempt to score a hole in one. The putter must "hole out" from each marker by picking up the ball from the hole, and starting again at the next marker. A student must complete one hole before moving on to another hole.
4. Scores are recorded on a student golf sheet.
5. If more than one student is playing from the same hole, individuals should alternate turns.
6. Teachers may substitute putting irons with field hockey sticks and balls when golf equipment is not available.
7. The object is to be the player with the lowest score at the completion of all 12 holes.
8. Self-Reflection Question - Did I hurry my shots or did I demonstrate patience in my strokes and interactions with classmates?

UNO PARED HANDBALL (PELOTO)

Spain

OUTCOME

Exhibit courtesy during game play

DESCRIPTION OF PLAY

Handball may be the oldest game played with a ball. The word *handball* appeared in ancient Egyptian and Greek literature. In France the game is called *Jeu de Paume,* and it is called *Peloto* in Spain. Handball was brought to America in 1886 by Irish immigrants with the first courts built in Brooklyn, New York. In Uno Pared Handball, partners alternate hitting a tennis ball against a wall.

PLAYING SPACE

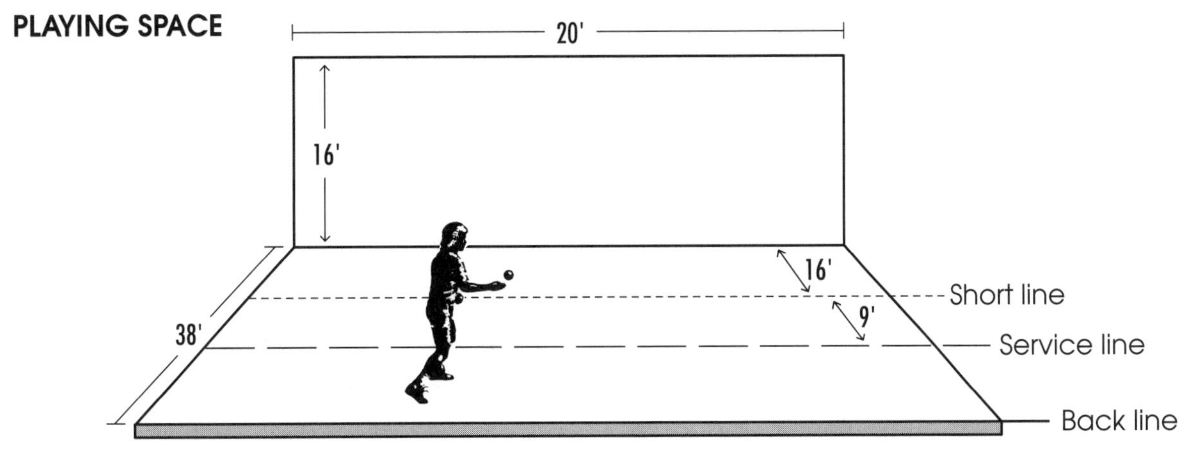

EQUIPMENT

Handballs or tennis balls and masking tape to line the courts

ESSENTIAL RULES FOR PLAY

1. Students should be encouraged to bring a close-fitting glove to class. Surgical or athletic tape may be worn around the hands beneath the gloves to prevent bruising. Partners should be asked to wrap each other's hands as a gesture of goodwill.
2. Play begins as one student stands between the short line and the service line and serves the ball by bouncing it on the floor, then hitting the ball so that it will strike the wall and rebound over the short line into the court.
3. The standard handball is made of black rubber and weighs 2.3 ounces. Pink Spaldeens™ or tennis balls can be used as a substitute.
4. The server is given two trials to serve the ball into the required playing area.
5. The two students continue to alternate hits.
6. A student must not interfere with his or her opponent's efforts at returning the ball. Blocking or pushing will result in a side out or penalty point. Unavoidable hinders

should be replayed.

7. The student can only score a point when he or she is serving. If the server loses the point, play continues with the other student serving.
8. Individuals agree to play to 10, 15, or 20 points.
9. Self-Reflection Question - Did I consistently serve the ball so that it hit the wall and rebounded over the short line into the court for my partner? Did I make every effort not to interfere with my partner's return of the ball?
10. Extension - Codeball (USA) uses the rules and playing space of handball with a 6-inch inflated ball that is kicked with the foot. To begin, the server stands in back of the service line, drops the ball, and kicks it on the first or second bounce. On the rebound, the kicked ball must cross the short line before striking the floor. The opposing player (or players in doubles) may return the ball by kicking it on the fly, first, or second bounce. No use of the hands, arms, or body is permitted. In a peer practice session, groups of five students can work cooperatively to kick ten consecutive kicks off the wall.

HAND TENNIS

OUTCOME

Enjoy friendly competition

Ireland

DESCRIPTION OF PLAY

It is a recognized historical fact that handball was first known in Ireland as the Game of Fives because players hit the ball with all five fingers. Hand tennis involves partners hitting a tennis ball back and forth over a neutral area using the hands. Students may use an underhand serve, a forehand, volley, or smash to alternate hits.

PLAYING SPACE

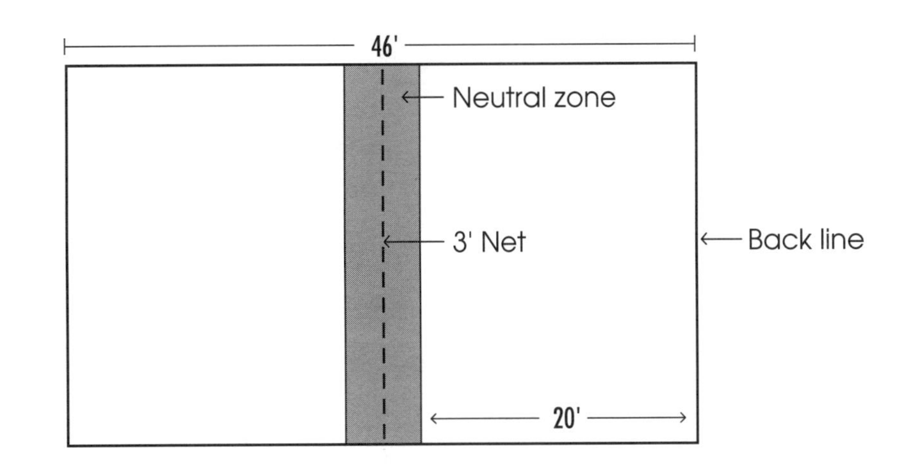

EQUIPMENT

3-foot net, measuring tapes, masking tape, tennis balls, and chalk

ESSENTIAL RULES FOR PLAY

1. Partners use a measuring tape and chalk to create the court. Two wooden chairs with a strip of masking tape attached to the top back of each chair can substitute for a 3-foot net.
2. Play begins when the student uses an underhand serve from behind the backline.
3. Scoring is only possible if the student is serving.
4. Both students continue to volley the ball until one or the other is unable to return it into the receiving area.
5. Balls can not be served or played in the neutral zone.
6. Individuals agree to play to 10, 15, or 20 points.
7. Self-Reflection Question - Which techniques do I need to practice in order to improve my performance, and continue to play other classmates?

EL CIRCULO HANDBALL

OUTCOME

Display ambition

DESCRIPTION OF PLAY

In 1050, French monks played *jeu de paume,* which meant hitting a ball with the palm of the hand. In Scotland, King James I blocked a window in his castle that interfered with his game of handball. Before becoming president, Abraham Lincoln played handball in a vacant street lot near his law office. El Circulo Handball uses the skills of serving, volleying, smashing, and the forehand stroke to hit a tennis ball so that it is placed inside a circular playing area. Partners volley the tennis ball until one student makes it impossible for the other student to return the ball.

PLAYING SPACE

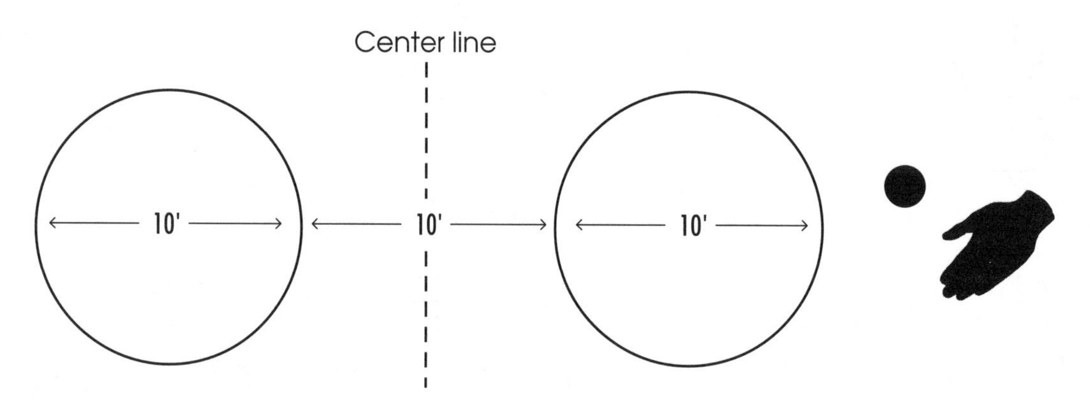

EQUIPMENT

Measuring tape, string, chalk, and handballs or tennis balls

ESSENTIAL RULES FOR PLAY

1. Partners use a measuring tape, string, and chalk to create the circle court.
2. Play begins with two students standing on opposite sides of the circular court, both positioned outside the circle.
3. One student uses an underhand serve to put the tennis ball in play.
4. The ball must land inside the circle on the serve and throughout the game.
5. Neither student may cross the center line to return the ball.
6. Scoring is only possible from the serve.
7. The service changes sides after each five points.
8. Individuals must agree to play to 10, 15, or 20 points.

9. Extension - In Partner El Circulo Handball, two partners challenge another set of partners by rotating in and out of the circle after every hit. For example, one individual serves to the opposite circle, then quickly steps out of the circle so that his or her partner can jump in and receive a returned hit.

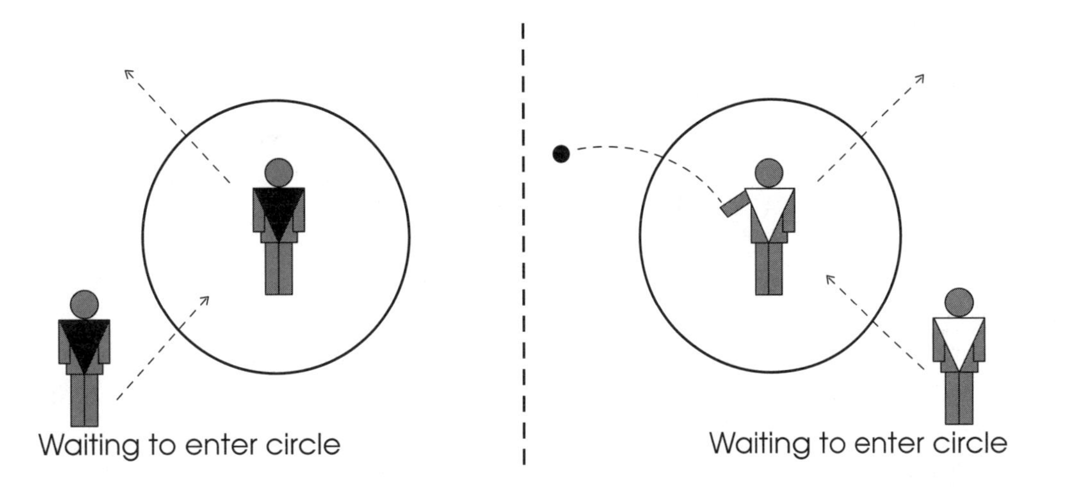

10. Self-Reflection Question - Did I maintain my efforts throughout the game, or did I allow my partner to easily defeat me?

SIDEWALK TENNIS

OUTCOME

Enjoy mutual play

DESCRIPTION OF PLAY

The Egyptians, Greeks, and Arabs all played a game similar to modern-day tennis. The sport of lawn tennis was brought to the United States in the late 1870s by Mary Ewing Outerbridge. In this French activity, partners hit a tennis ball back and forth over the center line of a sidewalk court.

PLAYING SPACE

20'

A	B	C	D
5'	5'	5'	5'

5'

EQUIPMENT

Measuring tapes, tennis balls, and chalk or shoe polish

ESSENTIAL RULES FOR PLAY

1. Partners use a measuring tape and chalk to create the court. Lines B and C divide the court and represent imaginary nets.
2. Play begins with one student dropping the ball in his or her back court (A or D) and having it land in the partner's front court. A served ball must bounce once before it can be played.
3. After the serve, the ball can land in either the front or back court and can be volleyed or hit on the first bounce. The hand must be kept open and the ball hit in the palm at all times.
4. After five serves, the service changes to the second player.
5. Students agree to play to 11, 16, or 21 points.
6. Self-Reflection Question - Did I show excitement when an extended rally occurred in the game?

CIRCLE PADDLE TENNIS

China

OUTCOME

Recognize the need for self-restraint

DESCRIPTION OF PLAY

It wasn't until the early 1900s that lightweight celluloid balls and rubber-pimpled paddles were used to play ping pong. The first championship took place in London and later China, Japan, and Korea transformed the game by adding great speed. Played in China, two students hit a tennis ball (or some other small ball) back and forth between two circles with a small hand paddle. The circles on the ground substitute for the ping pong (Ping-pang-chiu) table on many school grounds in China today.

PLAYING SPACE

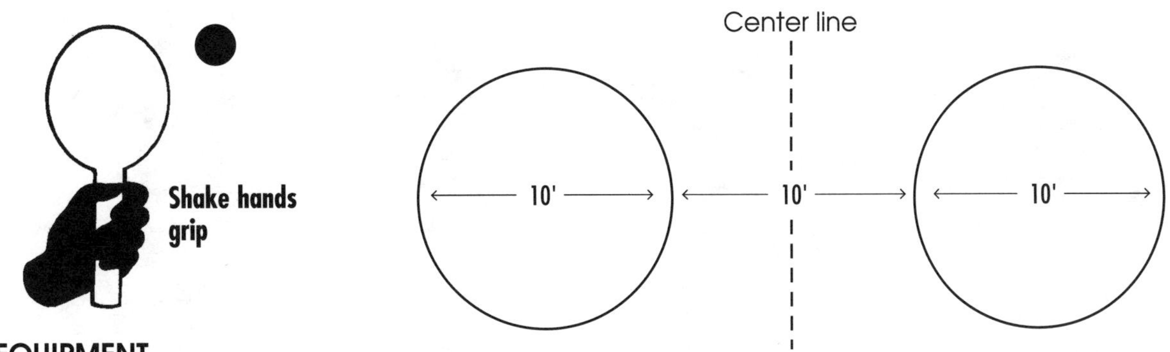

EQUIPMENT

Small hand paddles and tennis balls

ESSENTIAL RULES FOR PLAY

1. Partners use a measuring tape and chalk to create the court.
2. Partners conduct a peer practice session to determine the force needed to strike the ball into each other's circle. They practice by using the shake hands grip, which is the most common, and the pen holder grip. A pen holder grip, also called *Asian grip,* is when the paddle is held with the thumb and forefinger wrapped around the base of the handle and pressing from the forward surface against the other fingers on the non-striking side.
3. Play begins when one student drops the ball and serves underhand to his or her opponent's circle.
4. Overhand smashes are not permitted. There is a penalty of one point for this action.
5. Service changes after every five points.
6. Partners agree to play for 16 or 21 points. In the event that the score is 15-15 or 20- 20 (or deuce), the students should continue to play until there is a two point advantage.
7. Self-Reflection Question - Did I maintain control throughout the game, and resist smashing the ball when I had the opportunity?

FOOTBAG FEATS

OUTCOME

Display persistence

DESCRIPTION OF PLAY

Footbag has its roots in China. It was played in 2600 B.C. with a leather ball stuffed with hair. In the early 1970s, John Stalberger and Mike Marshall from the USA enjoyed kicking a stuffed sock back and forth which they later called "hacking the stack." In 1979, Stalberger patented the object as a "hackey sack." In 1983, the World Footbag Association (WFA) was formed to promote competition. Today, India is one of the world's largest manufacturers of footbags. In this activity, each student performs a series of footbag kicks while focusing on the center of the footbag.

PLAYING AREA

Inside

Outside

Thigh

Toe

EQUIPMENT

Footbags

ESSENTIAL RULES FOR PLAY

1. Individuals begin working with the footbag by imagining that a line separates the left side of the body from the right side.
2. The center of gravity should be kept low by bending the support leg and staying on the balls of the feet.
3. Each kick should be maintained at knee level.
4. The footbag may be kicked on the inside of the foot, by the knee raised to the mid-section of the body, by the toe, or by the foot behind the body if the footbag's flight extends outside range of the student's shoulders.
5. Peer practice sessions should focus on each partner kicking the footbag three or more times in succession. Begin by asking partners to toss the footbag to each other, and then progressing to kicking it to each other.
6. Self-Reflection Question - Was I persistent in trying to see the imaginary line that divides the body?
7. Extension - *Ch'ieh Tze* (Kee-uh-dsuh), or Chinese Shuttlecock, involves two or more students working together to keep a badminton shuttlecock in the air by using the skills common to footbag kicking.

JUMBLE JUGGLING

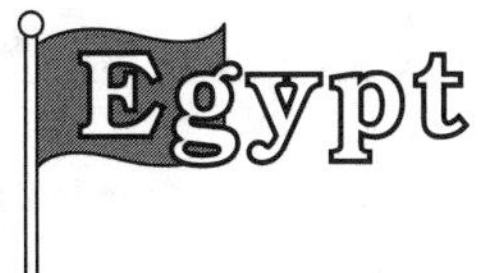

OUTCOME

Respond favorably to suggestions

DESCRIPTION OF PLAY

The first drawings of juggling appeared on Egyptian tombs around 2000 B.C. Asian performers piqued interest in the West while performing in English and US theaters and circuses in the early 1900s. Today, the International Jugglers Association oversees a long list of technical skills involving rings, balls, clubs, and even cigar boxes. Students of all ages feel a great sense of accomplishment when they can successfully juggle scarves, bean bags, or tennis balls. In this activity, individuals are encouraged to observe and correct a partner's movements when practicing the skills.

PLAYING SPACE

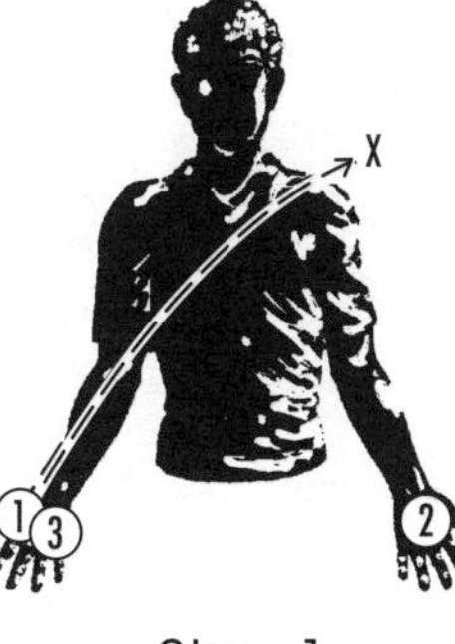

Step 1

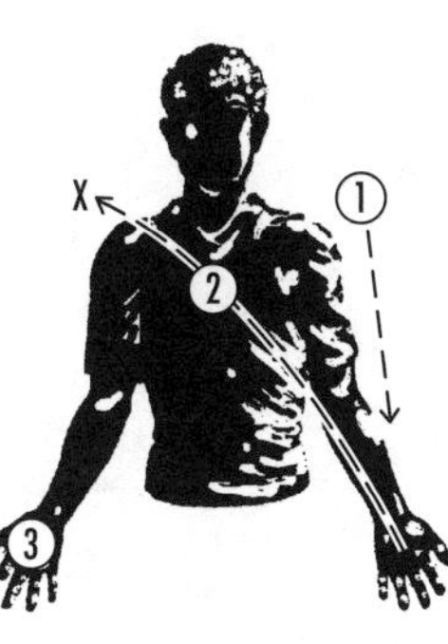

Step 2

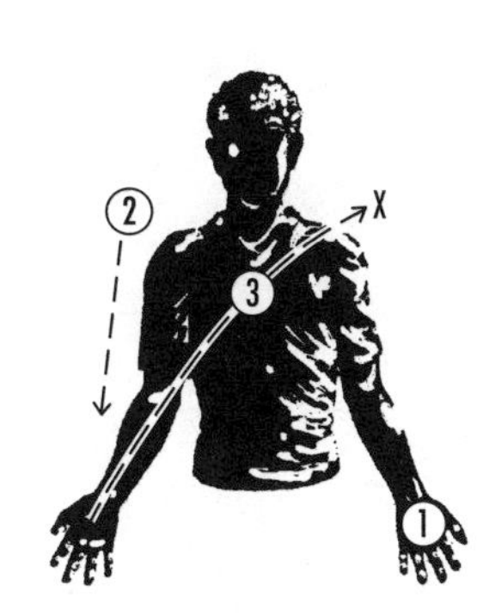

Step 3

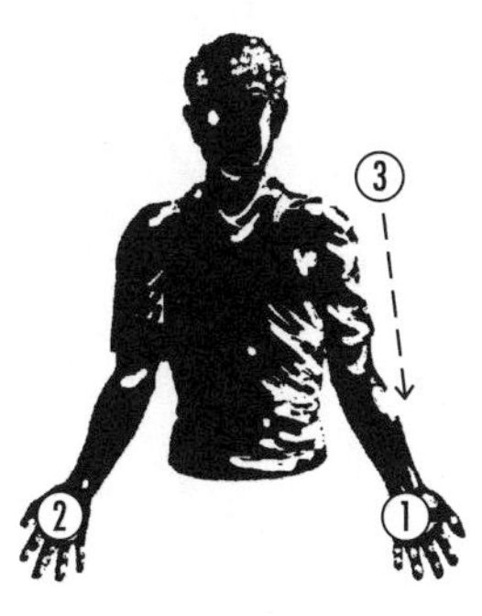

Step 4

EQUIPMENT

Juggle scarves, bean bags, or tennis balls

ESSENTIAL RULES FOR PLAY

1. Students begin by holding one ball in each hand.
2. The sequence is to toss one ball up using the right hand slightly above the left shoulder.
3. The elbows should be tucked in at waist level, and the wrists are flexible in order to catch the ball.
4. As the first ball descends, the ball held in the left hand is tossed up to the spot above the right shoulder.
5. Students should practice this toss several times to establish a smooth pattern. The sequence is repeated with the left hand.
6. A third ball is added to one of the hands. Begin with two balls in one hand and one in the other. The ball is tossed slightly higher.

7. Students should toss the third ball out of the hand quickly (i.e., just as the first ball is descending, and the second has reached its apex). One ball should be in the air at all times while a ball is being tossed.
8. The learning process will differ for individuals. A student should repeat the toss until he or she discovers a natural rhythm. During peer practice, partners should observe each other's juggling skills to assess the appropriate toss, height of the ball, and sequence of the toss.
9. Whenever possible, establish stations at the perimeters of the playing space. Each station should have a different type of juggling apparatus such as beanbags, rings, or regulation juggling balls. Partners rotate to each station and experiment with the additional equipment.
10. Self-Reflection Question - Did I accept my partner's suggestions regarding how high to toss the ball?
11. Extension - The Japanese juggling game *Otadama* challenges the individual to keep four or more objects in the air.

SHUFFLECURL

OUTCOME

Gain self-confidence

DESCRIPTION OF PLAY

Shuffleboard had great popularity in England during the Middle Ages. It was brought to America in the 1870s and was popular as a shipboard sport on ocean liners. Curling is a favorite winter sport of the English, German, and Canadian people. The sport of curling involves a curling stone referred to as a *rock*, brooms to sweep frost from the ice runway, and a marked target referred to as the *house*. Shufflecurl consists of a series of targets taped on the floor. Students standing 25 to 30 feet from a target slide a shufflecurl block to a designated target. Scores are recorded on individual worksheets.

PLAYING SPACE

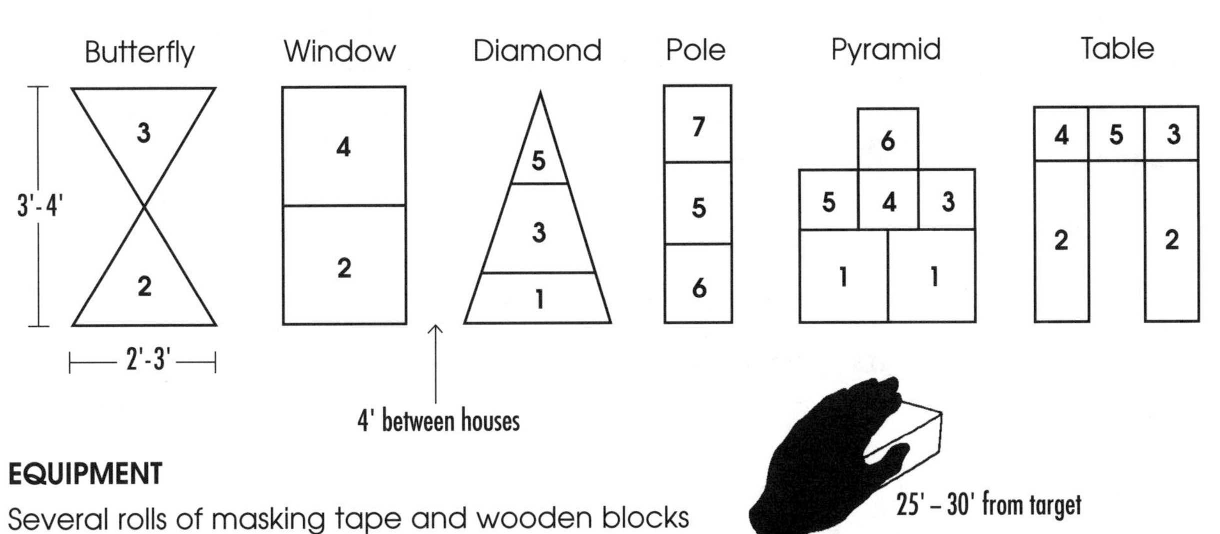

EQUIPMENT

Several rolls of masking tape and wooden blocks

ESSENTIAL RULES FOR PLAY

1. Students use measuring tape and masking tape to create the six "house" targets on a smooth floor, and an endline 25 to 30 feet opposite the targets. The size of the targets can vary between 3 to 4 feet depending on the distance. If possible, leave a minimum of 4 feet between each target.
2. Students must use their hand and a pushing motion to propel the block toward the house.
3. Each student slides two shufflecurl blocks at each house, returns the shufflecurl to the endline, and records his or her score on the worksheet.
4. The combined score for the eight targets is recorded under trial 1.
5. Students are challenged to complete trials 1 through 3 before comparing scores with classmates.
6. Self-Reflection Question - Did my score improve in trial 2?

SHUFFLECURL STUDENT WORKSHEET

NAME(S) ____

INSTRUCTIONS

You should find 2 shufflecurl blocks at each house's endline. Total your score for each target. Combine all six scores for a grand total score. If the targets do not include the numbers, you may refer to this worksheet.

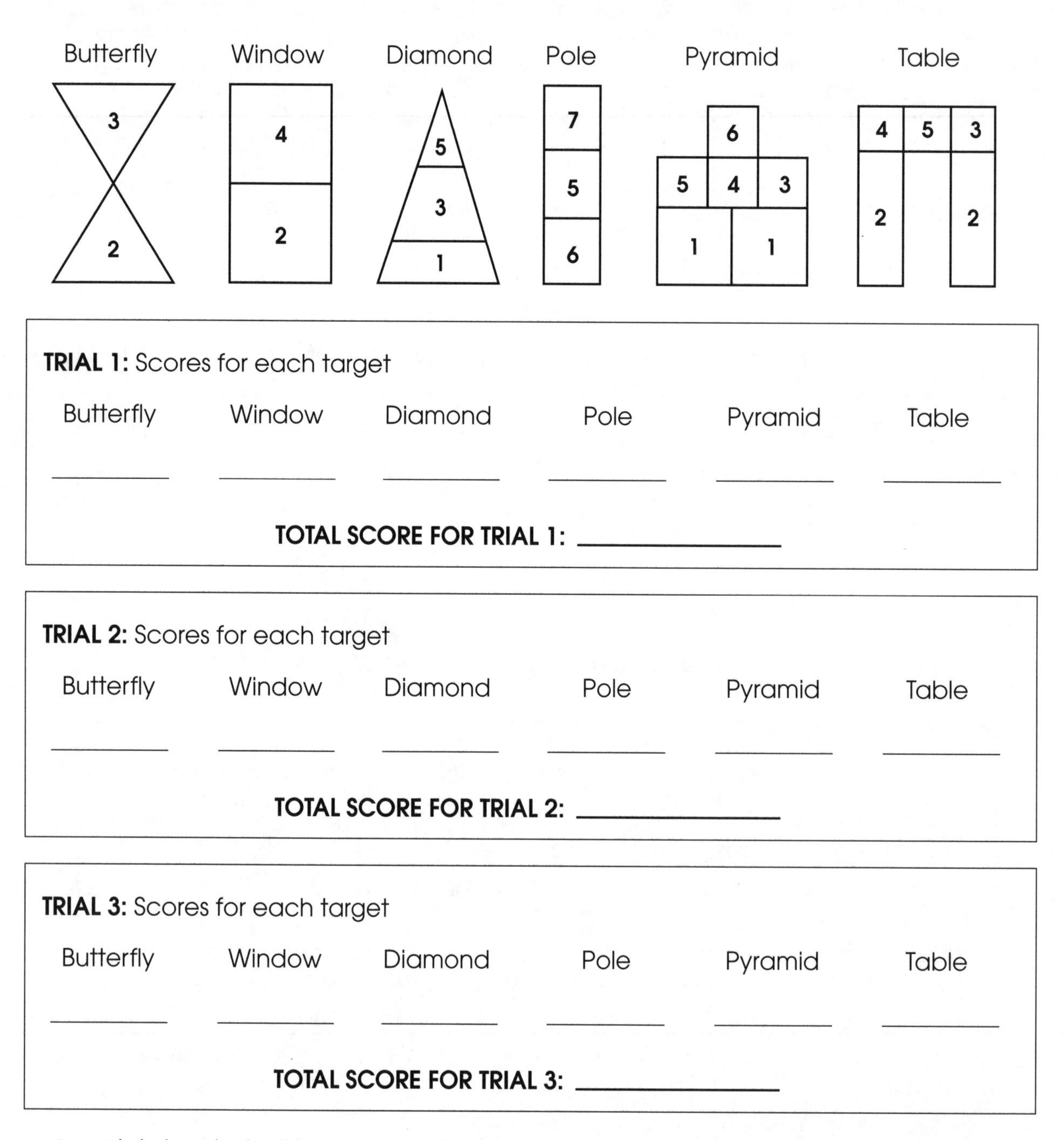

TRIAL 1: Scores for each target

Butterfly	Window	Diamond	Pole	Pyramid	Table
________	________	________	________	________	________

TOTAL SCORE FOR TRIAL 1: ______________

TRIAL 2: Scores for each target

Butterfly	Window	Diamond	Pole	Pyramid	Table
________	________	________	________	________	________

TOTAL SCORE FOR TRIAL 2: ______________

TRIAL 3: Scores for each target

Butterfly	Window	Diamond	Pole	Pyramid	Table
________	________	________	________	________	________

TOTAL SCORE FOR TRIAL 3: ______________

BOCCIE SOFTBALL

Italy

OUTCOME

Judge results fairly

DESCRIPTION OF PLAY

Derived from the Romans, this popular Italian and French game (*Boules* or *Petanque* where metal balls are lobbed at the target instead of rolled along the ground) is typically played on a 10-foot by 76-foot hard dirt court, enclosed by wooden boards measuring 10 to 12 inches at the sides. "Boccie" became very popular in Italy during the 19th century and was brought to the USA by Italian immigrants. Boccie Softball can be played on a school yard or in the hallway by using mats and painted softballs. The game is played by throwing a "jack" ball into a specific playing area. Boccie softballs are then thrown by team players to see who can get closest to the jack. The scoring in this modified version is similar to the American game of horseshoes.

PLAYING SPACE

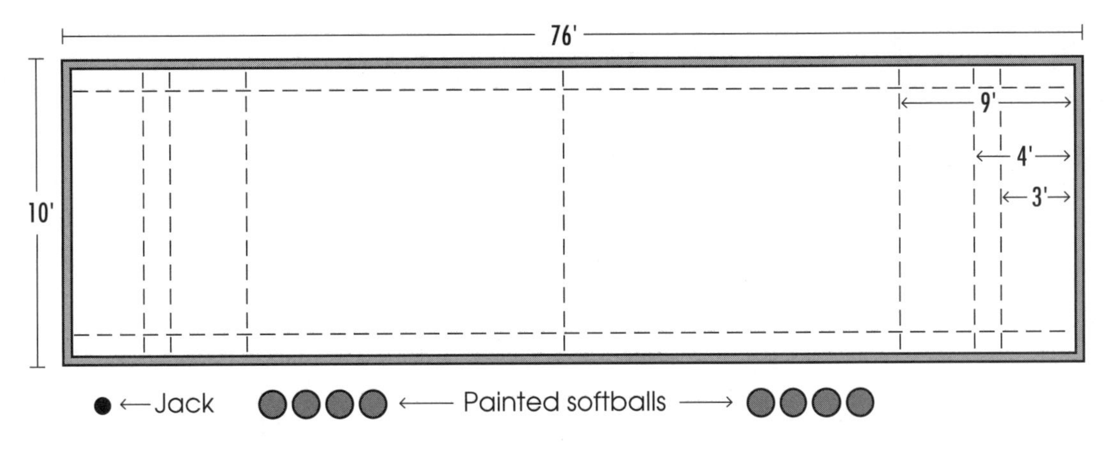

EQUIPMENT

Used softballs, one golf ball, spray paint or coloring markers

ESSENTIAL RULES FOR PLAY

1. Partners work together to play opposing partners or teams. The typical team consists of four players per boccie court.
2. Each team is given four boccie balls, which are normally 4-1/2 inches in diameter. Used softballs may be spray painted or numbered to distinguish between teams when actual boccie balls are not available.
3. Each team is given a "jack" ball, which is typically 2 to 3 inches in diameter. Small hard superballs or golf balls can be substituted.
4. A student from one team tosses the jack toward the opposite end of the court for positioning. He or she then rolls or tosses underhand one of the boccie softballs as

close to the jack as possible. One opposing player then throws a ball in turn, to see which of them is closer to the jack. The team with the player who is closest to the jack takes its turn.

5. After a team has used all of the balls, the opposing team "bowls" its remaining balls. The balls must be thrown underhand. They may also be tossed or rolled.
6. It is legal to move the jack with a bowl, or to knock an opponent's ball away from the jack.
7. A team receives one point for each ball closer to the jack than the opposing team's closest ball. Teams agree to play to 8, 10, or the regulation 12 points.
8. Self-Reflection Question - Did I accept my opponent's calculation of the points at the end of the game?

RUSSIAN GORODRI

OUTCOME

Appreciate unfamiliar activities

DESCRIPTION OF PLAY

Gorodri is a highly recognized game in Russia. In this modified version, students use a 3-foot stick to knock over wooden pegs that have been placed in a particular formation within a designated area.

PLAYING SPACE

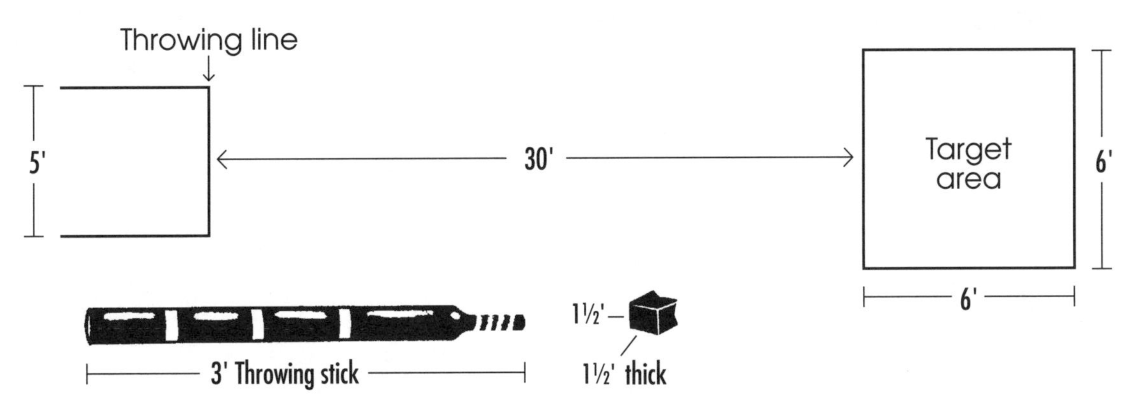

EQUIPMENT

Five 8-inch wooden dowels, two 3-foot long wooden throwing sticks. Rolled newspaper with 3-foot dowel rod in the center taped so that it is a throwing stick, and tin cans for pegs can also be used

WOODEN PEG FORMATION

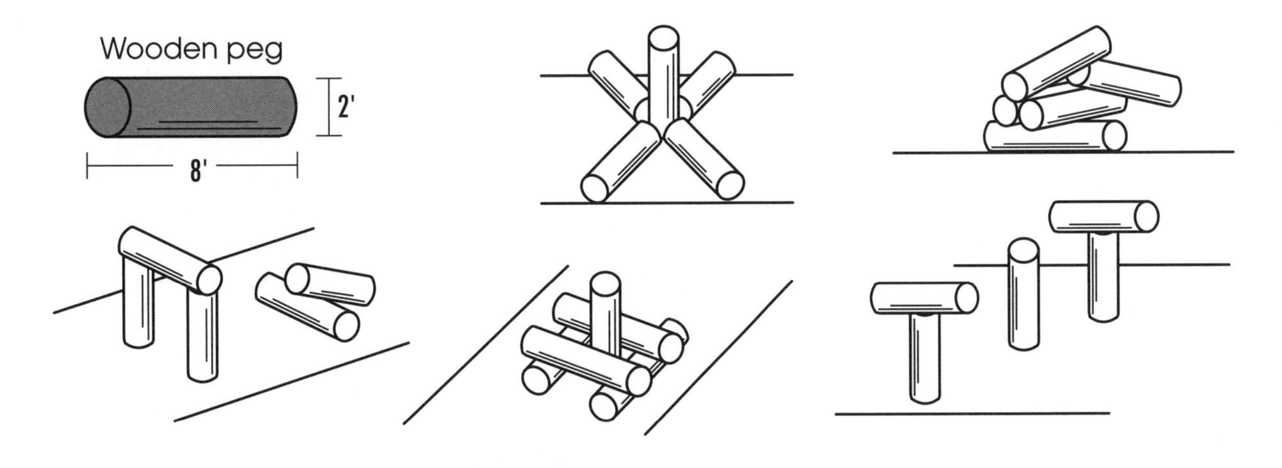

ESSENTIAL RULES FOR PLAY

1. The game is played with partners or small groups.
2. Students use a sidearm throw in their attempts at hitting the pegs.
3. Individuals are allowed two throws to knock the pegs completely out of the square. Each peg counts as one point. A peg that is touching a line is not counted as being out.
4. If a student knocks all five pegs out of the box on the first throw, he or she receives a score of five. The next player takes a turn after the pegs have been reset. Students take turns setting the pegs in an agreed-upon formation.
5. If one or more pegs remain in the box after the first attempt, the student is allowed a second throw. At that time, the score is recorded and the pegs are reset.
6. Self-Reflection Question - Did I listen carefully to the rules so as not to delay play at the beginning of the game, and use a side arm throw?

SOFT TOSS HORSESHOES

OUTCOME

Derive pleasure from leisure activities

DESCRIPTION OF PLAY

Horseshoe pitching was brought to England by Roman soldiers from Italy, where it became very popular. The game came to America with the first colonists and developed into a competitive game. President Harry S. Truman pitched horseshoes on the lawn of the White House. In this activity, students pitch rubber horseshoes at stakes that are either driven into the ground, or attached to rubber mats and placed on a gymnastic mat.

PLAYING SPACE

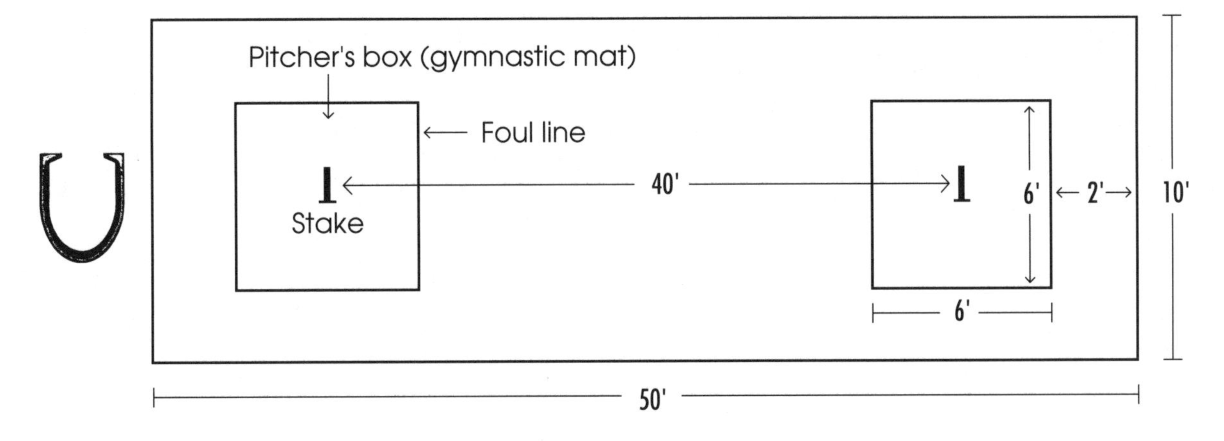

EQUIPMENT

Measuring tapes, horseshoes, and iron stakes or rubber mat horseshoe targets

ESSENTIAL RULES FOR PLAY

1. Partners design the playing area. Each student is given two horseshoes. Both players stand in the pitcher's box. The first student pitches both shoes. The student's feet must stay behind the foul line until the shoe has left the hand. The second student takes a turn.
2. In singles action, both students pitch the shoes and proceed to the opposite end. They total their score and pitch back at the other end.
3. In doubles, students do not walk to the opposite side. Instead, they wait for the other students to pitch shoes, after which they pitch them back.
4. In either singles or doubles, one student pitches both shoes before the other has a turn.
5. The score is determined by the positions of the shoes after all four shoes have been

pitched. The shoe that is closest to the stake scores one point. If both shoes thrown by one student are closer than his or her opponent, the student is given two points. A ringer is a shoe that encircles the stake. A ringer equals three points. A shoe that leans against the stake equals one point.

6. A score is not normally counted unless the shoe is within 6 inches of the stake. This decision should be made before the game begins.
7. Horseshoes have curved edges called *Heel Calks* and a raised *Toe Calk* for gripping at the center.
8. Students agree to play to 15, 21, or 50 points, and may decide to decrease the length from stake to stake to 30 feet.
9. Self-Reflection Question - Did I participate whole-heartedly and express enjoyment in learning the rules to horseshoes?

SKIDDLES

Belgium

OUTCOME

Aspire to new challenges

DESCRIPTION OF PLAY

Originating in Europe, Skiddles is an ancient target game that makes use of three throwing sticks and five pins to reach a score of 100 points. Belgium hosts many recreational tournaments.

PLAYING SPACE

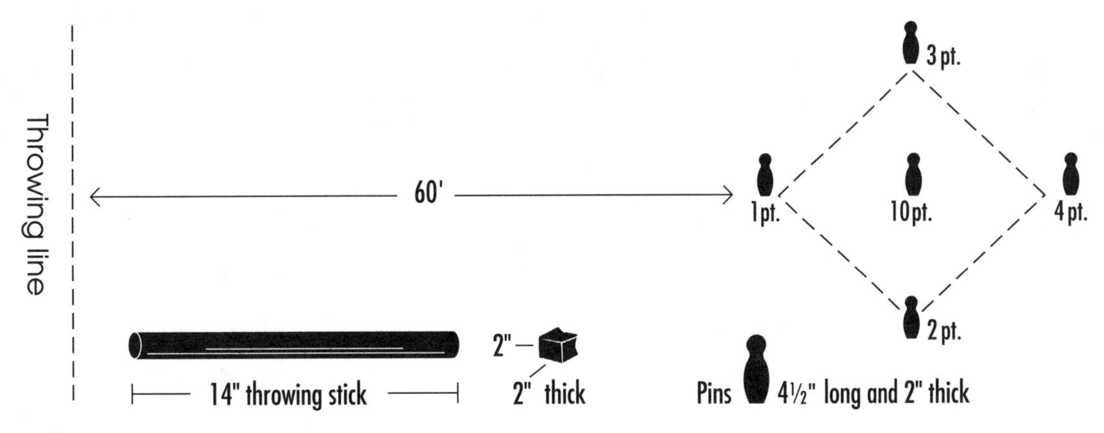

EQUIPMENT

Five bowling pins and three throwing sticks or wooden blocks

ESSENTIAL RULES FOR PLAY

1. The game is played with partners or small groups of students. Place a 4-1/2 inch pin (1-1/2 to 2 inches thick) in each corner of the 30-inch square, and one pin directly in the center of the target. Three throwing sticks (14 inches in length and 2 inches thick) are used to hit the pins. Equipment can be purchased in a local hardware store or the school's woodworking department.
2. Plastic bowling pins and a 14-foot by 2-foot piece of wood can be substituted if regulation equipment is not available.
3. Individuals take turns standing behind the throwing line and throw, in any desired manner, all three throwing sticks at the pins.
4. The score is determined as follows:
   - The pin nearest the throwing line = 1 point
   - The pin to the right = 2 points
   - The pin to the left = 3 points
   - The pin in the rear = 4 points
   - The center pin scores 10 points

5. Traditionally, the game is played to 100 points, with the rule that if a player goes over 100 points on the final throw, he or she must start from zero. Students are encouraged to conduct a forum to determine if the traditional rule will be maintained or the declared winner is the first player to reach 100 points after all members have had the same number of throws.
6. It is wise to mark the dot where the pins are set to assist in the resetting process.
7. The throwing is underhand, and the throwing player may not step over the throwing line.
8. The score is always the total number of pins knocked down.
9. Expert players tend to throw a stick so they either hit the ground and roll just before they strike the pin, or so that it is whirling when it contacts the ground in front of the pins.
10. Self-Reflection Question - Did I try to improve my skills after my first throw at the pins?
11. Extension - *English Skittles* - Place the pins in a "V" formation. From the throwing line, each player throws three throwing sticks or balls at the skittles. Five points are awarded for the farthest pin, three points each for the next farthest pins, and two points each for the closest pins. If all five are down before three throws are taken, they are erected again and the shots are completed. Players take turns until each player has had ten turns.

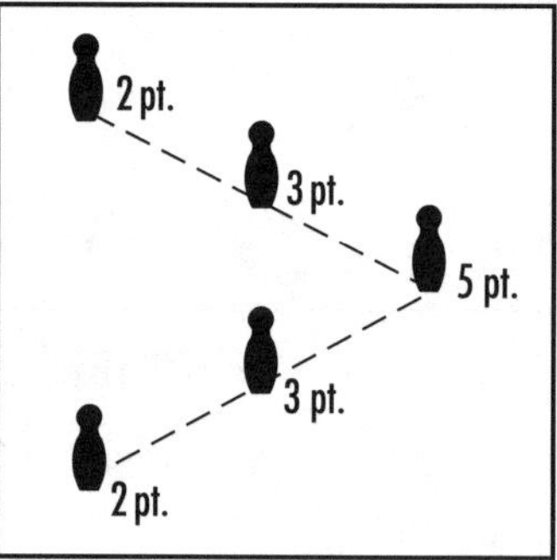

PARTNER CULTURALLY DIVERSE COMBATIVE CHALLENGES

International

OUTCOME

Compare physical abilities

DESCRIPTION OF PLAY

Combative challenges have existed in all cultures as a way to condition the body for greater health and physical ability. Abraham Lincoln was a wrestler before he became the President of the United States. The Asian culture used combative challenges in their martial arts training. In this activity, partners challenge each other's ability in combative tasks that emphasize pushing, pulling, reaction time, and strength. Individuals should select partners of similar body type and height, and shake hands before performing each challenge. Safety should be recognized.

PLAYING SPACE

English Dragon's Lair

EQUIPMENT

Gymnastic mats, if available, and balloons and strips of string for one challenge

ESSENTIAL RULES FOR PUSHING ACTIVITIES

PUSHING: To move something away by pressing or exerting force against it.

1. *Italian Push Away* - Partners stand facing each other approximately 2 feet apart with their palms touching. On the teacher's signal, each student pushes the other's palms in an attempt to make the opponent step back with one foot.
2. *Swedish Sawing Wood* - Partners stand facing each other on any line that is marked on the floor. Each partner's knees are slightly bent and the feet are pointing to the opposite player. On the teacher's signal, the students interlock fingers and raise the hands to chest height. While straddling the line, they start pumping their arms back and forth and imitate the action of sawing wood. The object is to remain on the line by resisting the other partner's efforts as he or she pushes the arms back and forth in a sawing motion.
3. *Luto de Galo* (Loo-tah day gahlo) - Rooster fighting is played in Brazil and Portugal, in which partners try to snatch a handkerchief (the rooster's tail) from the opponent's

back pocket while only using one hand and hopping on one foot. Individuals defend their own rooster tail by dodging and twisting.

4. *German Bulldozer* - Partners stand face-to-face with right shoulders touching. On the teacher's signal, both attempt to push the other in such a way that he or she steps backward.
5. *Chinese Hawk Flight* - Partners each raise their left foot and grasp it with their left hand from behind to hop on one leg. The right arm remains free but is bent at the elbow and placed behind the back. On the teacher's signal, both players enter a 6-foot circle, shake hands, and begin the challenge. The object is to push your partner outside the circle or to force the individual to step down.

ESSENTIAL RULES FOR PULLING ACTIVITIES

PULLING: To move apart by exerting force.

1. *Hand Tug of War* - Students stand facing each other. On the teacher's signal, each player extends his or her right hand forward and attempts to pull the other player toward the body until crossing an imaginary line.
2. *French Finger Fencing* - A student extends his or her right index finger and hooks it around the partner's right index finger. Students then grasp their own left ankle with their left hand so that both are balancing on one foot. The objective is to pull the partner in such a way that he or she will step down with both feet.
3. *American Indian Standing Hand Wrestle* - Partners stand facing each other with their right feet touching and their right hands clasped. On the teacher's signal, they attempt to pull each other forward until one causes the other to lift his or her back foot.

ESSENTIAL RULES FOR REACTION TIME CONTESTS

REACTION TIME: The ability to respond quickly and accurately.

1. *Japanese Knee Touch* - Partners attempt to touch or tap each other's knee before being tapped three times.
2. *Spanish Foot Tag* - Partners attempt to use their own feet to touch the feet of the other person before being touched three times.
3. *English Balloon Burst* - Partners each inflate a balloon and tie it to a 2-foot string. The end of the string is then tied to each student's left shoelace. The object is to step quickly and burst the other player's balloon.
4. *German Pushup Break Down* - Partners are face-to-face in a pushup position. The object is to cause the other person to break down by grasping the partner's arm in such a way that he or she cannot maintain the pushup position.
5. *English Hot Hands* - Partners stand facing each other. One student places his or her hands out in front of the body (palms facing downward). The other student places his or her hands behind the back. This student attempts to bring his/her hands around the body and slap the partner's hands. Each student has three attempts before the role changes.

ESSENTIAL RULES FOR STRENGTH ACTIVITIES

STRENGTH: To exert force for an extended period of time.

1. *American Indian Leg Wrestling* - Partners lie on a mat side-by-side with their feet in opposite directions. The hips of both students should be aligned. Partners interlock right arms. On the teacher's signal, the students raise inside legs until their toes touch. On a second signal, the action is repeated. On the third signal, the students hook legs and try to roll the partner over to his or her side of the mat.
2. *English Dragon's Lair* - Use chalk or tape to depict a 5-foot circle on the floor. The circle represents the "dragon's lair" or "mouth." Partners stand on opposite sides of the lair. On signal, both players run around the circle, meet, and have 30 seconds to try to pull or push the other's body into the dragon's mouth without having one's own body enter the circle.
3. *German Arm Wrestle* - Partners sit at a table facing each other. Each student uses the same arm, and locks hands with the partner. Elbows must remain on the table. The object is to force the partner's arm to the table.
4. *Greek Flip The Turtle* - One partner lies face down with legs and arms stretched outward to form a "turtle." The second player has 30 seconds to try to move or flip the player on to his or her back.
5. *Egyptian Tug of War* - One set of partners challenge another set of partners to an Egyptian Tug of War by first shaking hands. Individuals from each set of partners clasp their arms around the waist of their partner, and face the other two individuals. Both sets of partners stand over a line on the floor. The inside partners then grasp hands. Both sets of partners try to pull the other over the line.

HEARTY WORKOUTS

OUTCOME

Render goodwill toward a partner

DESCRIPTION OF PLAY

The Greek physician, Hippocrates (born about 460 B.C.), wrote, "All parts of the body have a function, if used in moderation and exercised in labours in which each is accustomed, become thereby healthy, well-developed and age more slowly; but if unused and left idle they become liable to disease, defective in growth, and age quickly." In this activity, partners take their pulse and participate in a series of exercises designed to raise the pulse rate. Students record their partner's pulse after each exercise and determine which exercise has the greatest effect on the heart.

PLAYING SPACE

EQUIPMENT

Stop watches or wrist watches, and worksheet

ESSENTIAL RULES FOR PLAY

1. During a peer practice session, each student should locate his or her pulse at the radial artery. To locate the radial pulse, use the sensitive tips of the index, middle, and ring fingers. Feel for the wristbone at the base of the thumb. Move the fingertips toward the wrist and feel for the pulse. After several trials, locating the pulse should become easier. Individuals should locate the radial pulse on both wrists.
2. Students should also locate the pulse at the carotid artery. To locate the carotid pulse, use the tips of the index, middle, and ring fingers. Feel for the jawbone at the top of the neck. Move the fingertips slightly down and toward the center of the neck and feel for the pulse. After several trials, this should become easier. Individuals should locate the carotid pulse on both sides of the neck.
3. One student records the results while his or her partner performs the task. Partners exchange roles when all tasks are completed. If at any time dizziness occurs during an exercise, the individual should stop immediately.

HEARTY WORKOUT PARTNER WORKSHEET

PARTNER 1 ____

PARTNER 2 ____

INSTRUCTIONS

1. Each student should locate his or her radial pulse and carotid artery.
2. One person records the results while the other student performs each of the seven tasks.
3. After both partners have had a turn, one partner charts his or her own results, followed by the second partner's results. Discuss your conclusion.
4. Sit quietly for 1 minute and record the pulse.

   Partner 1 ______________ Partner 2 ______________

5. Stand quietly for 1 minute and record the pulse.

   Partner 1 ______________ Partner 2 ______________

6. Jog in place for 1 minute and record the pulse. (Rest for 2 minutes to return heart rate to normal.)

   Partner 1 ______________ Partner 2 ______________

7. Perform two-count jumping jacks and jills for 1 minute and record the pulse. (Rest for 2 minutes.)

   Partner 1 ______________ Partner 2 ______________

8. Hop up and down for 1 minute and record the pulse. (Rest for 2 minutes.)

   Partner 1 ______________ Partner 2 ______________

9. Run vigorously in place for 1 minute and record the pulse. (Rest for 2 minutes.)

   Partner 1 ______________ Partner 2 ______________

10. Complete the activity by charting both partners' results on the following worksheet to assess the similarities and differences of each student's pulse rate.

PARTNER WORKSHEET FOR CHARTING PULSE RATE

PARTNER 1 ____

PARTNER 2 ____

INSTRUCTIONS

Place a dot above each activity to indicate the individual's pulse rate. After all dots are identified, draw a line from the sitting pulse rate to the standing pulse rate and so on to complete a graph. Answer questions A and B and discuss your findings with your partner.

200						
180						
160						
140						
120						
100						
80						
60						
	• Sitting	• Standing	• Jogging	• Jumping Jacks/Jills	• Hopping	• Running

A. The pulse rate was the lowest after 1 minute of (which activity)

Partner 1 ______________ Partner 2 ______________

B. The pulse rate was the highest after 1 minute of (which activity)

Partner 1 ______________ Partner 2 ______________

Self-Reflection Question - Which activity can I use in the future to increase my level of physical activity?

From *A Multicultural Approach to Physical Education: Proven Strategies for Middle and High School* by Rhonda L. Clements and Suzanne K. Kinzler, 2003, Champaign, IL: Human Kinetics

JUST BE NIMBLE JUMP

Denmark

OUTCOME

Reveal qualities of self-determination

DESCRIPTION OF PLAY

Drawings of children jumping over the linked arms of other children were found dating back as far as 3300 B.C. in Egypt. This Danish activity involves jumping in the formation of a hexagon (a six-sided shape) to increase one's level of physical fitness.

PLAYING SPACE

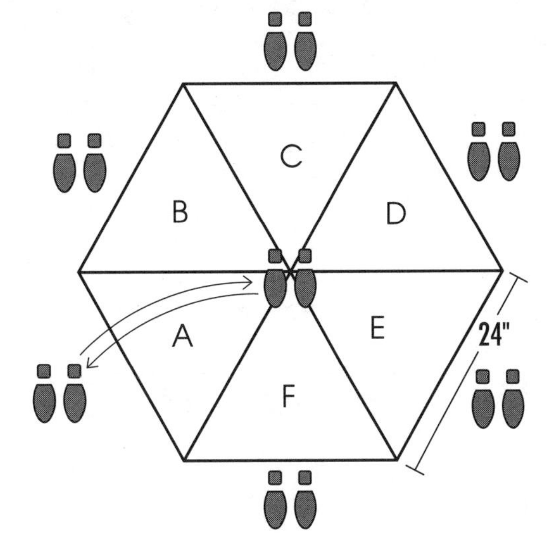

EQUIPMENT

Masking tape, measuring tapes, stop watches or wrist watches

ESSENTIAL RULES FOR PLAY

1. Partners use masking tape and measuring tape to create a hexagon. Each of the six sides should equal 2 feet.
2. One student records the result while his or her partner performs the task. Partners exchange roles when the task is completed.
3. Starting Position: Stand facing side F.
4. Action: Jump to the outside of side A and back to center. Jump to the outside of side B and back to center. Jump to the outside of side C and back to center, etc. THE JUMPER SHOULD ALWAYS BE FACING SIDE F. Complete the circuit three times.
5. Scoring for this task should be as follows:
   - Completing the circuit three times in less than 12 seconds – SUPER!
   - Completing the circuit three times in less than 17 seconds – GOOD JOB!
   - Completing the circuit three times in less than 22 seconds – HEAVY FEET!
   - Completing the circuit three times in greater than 25 seconds – MAYBE NEXT TIME!
6. Self-Reflection Question - Did I continue to perform at my best throughout all three trials?

WALK BEFORE YOU RUN

International

OUTCOME

Accept constructive feedback

DESCRIPTION OF PLAY

The earliest message runners from the Empire of the Incas were called *chasqui (chas-kee).* They developed excellent running styles between the 2-mile posts, and were brightly dressed to be easily seen by watchers. Foot races conducted in ancient Greece were probably the first track events. Modern track events that emphasize running include sprinting, middle distance events, distance events, relays, hurdles, and walking races. Carl Lewis, Michael Johnson, Evelyn Ashford, Jackie Joyner-Kersee, and Grete Waitz are well known for their speed and endurance in Olympic running events. In this activity, partners perform the techniques of fitness walking, jogging, and running, and observe each other's performance to suggest corrections.

PLAYING SPACE

Partners facing posters taped on wall for easy viewing

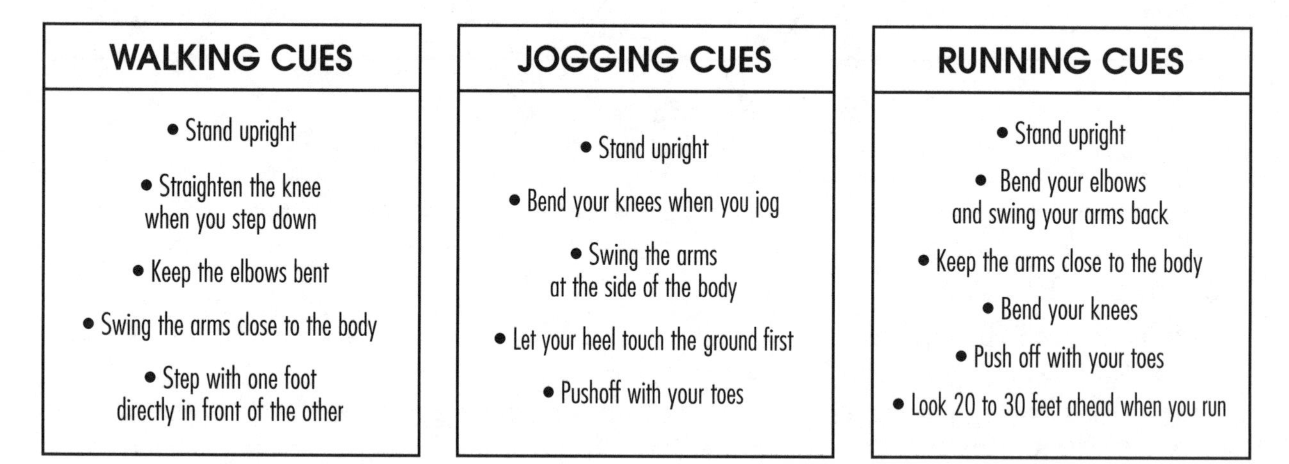

EQUIPMENT

Posters with walking, jogging, and running cues for all students to view easily

ESSENTIAL RULES FOR PLAY

1. Partners perform the following tasks: one student will read the cues and observe his or her partner's performance for correct form. Partners exchange roles when all tasks are completed.
2. Explain that fitness walking involves moving at a fast pace. With each step, the leading foot must make contact with the ground before the trailing foot leaves the ground. During each step, the knee must be straightened with the body carried in an upright position. The elbows are bent at 90-degree angles. The arms swing close to

the body at all times. Practice walking on a straight line.

3. Discuss how jogging involves running at a slow pace. There is a very brief period of time when both feet are off the ground at the same time. The arms are carried comfortably at about 90-degree angles. The arms should not cross the midline of the body. The body is carried in an upright position. Each foot lands on the ground with the heel striking first followed by the pushoff with the toes.
4. Reinforce that running involves moving at a quicker pace than jogging. There is a very brief period of time when both feet are off the ground at the same time. The arms are carried at about 90-degree angles. The arms should not cross the midline of the body. The body is carried in an upright position. Each foot should land on the ground with the heel to middle of the foot striking the ground first and the pushoff is with the toes.
5. Using the basic fitness walking technique, individuals move from one end of the workout area to the opposite side and return. Repeat three times.
6. Using the basic jogging technique, individuals move from one end of the workout area to the opposite side and return. Repeat three times.
7. Using the basic running technique, individuals move from one end of the workout area to the opposite side and return. Repeat two times.
8. Self-Reflection Question – How quickly did I respond to my partner's suggestions?
9. Extension – Walk, Jog, or Run for Fun involves moving for a period of 12 minutes using a combination of fitness walking, jogging, and running.

   Note: All students should move in the same direction during this activity.

WEIGHTLESS WORKOUTS

OUTCOME

Take initiative to accomplish a task

DESCRIPTION OF PLAY

In ancient times, weight training was believed to carry no benefits and result in poor flexibility. Women were not encouraged to lift weights because a strong physique on a woman was considered to be vulgar. It was not until the 1920s, when physical therapists used weight training techniques to rehabilitate a soldier's leg and arm injuries, that people began using dumbbells, barbells, and pulley systems to improve their fitness levels and appearance. In the following series of activities, partners use a towel or strips of tire inner tubes to strengthen and tone the body's muscles.

PLAYING SPACE

EQUIPMENT

Towels or strips of tire inner tubes

ESSENTIAL RULES FOR PLAY

1. Partners should find a space on the floor where they can work comfortably and safely.
2. One student observes his or her partner's performance while the other person follows the teacher's instruction, and then they switch.
3. High Five! Each partner should perform five repetitions of each exercise. If the exercise involves using opposite body parts, individuals should perform five repetitions on each body part.
4. If the exercise is a stretch, individuals should hold the stretch for at least 5 seconds. All stretches should be performed slowly while breathing naturally.

A. PULLDOWNS

Starting Position: Stand with the feet apart and the hands holding each end of the towel. The towel should be stretched out above the head with the elbows slightly bent.

Action: While pulling at both ends of the towel, slowly bend the elbows and lower the towel behind the head. Raise the towel back to the starting position.

B. SIDE STRETCHES

Starting Position: Hold the towel stretched behind the head with the elbows slightly bent. Keep the feet shoulder width apart.

Action: Lean as far to the right as possible and hold the position for 5 seconds. Lean to the left as far as possible and hold for 5 seconds.

C. LEG STRETCH

Starting Position: Sit with one leg extended forward and one leg bent with the foot against the opposite knee. Wrap the towel around the ball of the foot of the straight leg and hold it with both hands.

Action: Slowly lean forward at the waist and hold the position. Use the towel to pull the upper body forward. Repeat the movement with the other leg.

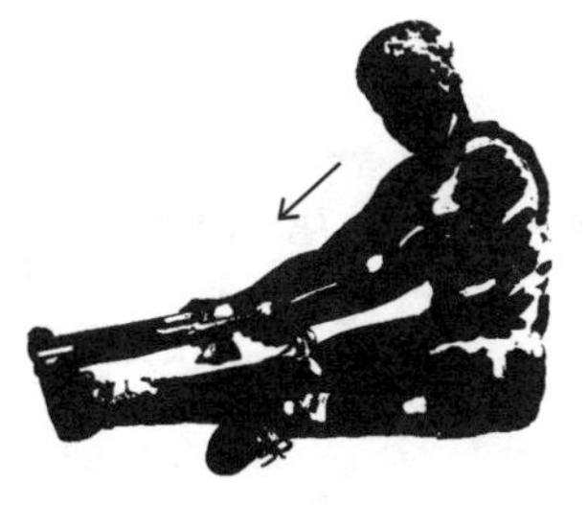

D. UPPER BACK STRETCH

Starting Position: Stand with the feet shoulder width apart. Hold one end of the towel behind the head with the elbow of one arm bent. Reach up with the other hand to hold on to the other end of the towel.

Action: Slowly move the lower hand up the towel so that the upper arm is pulled downward. Try to touch the hands and hold the position. Repeat the action with the other arm.

PARTNER CULTURALLY DIVERSE FITNESS ACTIVITIES

International

OUTCOME

Experience cultural diversity through fitness activities

DESCRIPTION OF PLAY

In the following activities, partners participate in a variety of fitness tasks originating from culturally diverse populations.

PLAYING SPACE

Russian Cossack Kicks

EQUIPMENT

Foam balls, wooden dowels, and 16-foot-long jump rope

ESSENTIAL RULES FOR PLAY

1. *American Indian Footraces* - Partners run a "30-mile course" in the gymnasium. Each lap of the gymnasium symbolizes one mile.
2. *Mexican Plima* - Partners stand 15 to 20 feet apart while facing each other. One student is given a foam ball. The objective is to avoid being hit by the thrown ball by dodging, ducking, and leaping into the air. Partners exchange roles after five throws. The activity is completed when one student successfully dodges 20 throws.
3. *Japanese Pushups* - To perform a judo/karate pushup, the student will bend his or her body in a V-shape, with hands and feet on the floor and knees slightly bent. The student slowly rises up on the toes, bends at the elbow, and arches the body forward with the head up and then returns to the starting position. One student will perform ten pushups while his or her partner counts to ten in Japanese.

   1 = *ichi (itchy)* 2 = *ni (knee)* 3 = *san (sun)* 4 = *shi (shi)* 5 = *go (go)*

   6 = *roko (rocko)* 7 = *shichi (shi-chi)* 8 = *hachi (hat-chi)* 9 = *kyu (coo)* 10 = *ju (ju)*
4. *Russian Cossack Kicks* - To perform a Cossack kick, the student lowers the hips in close proximity to the floor. The back should be straight. The knees should be bent and under the hips. The student pushes on the toes and kicks one leg out in front of the body to touch the heel on the floor. The student changes legs and continues the action until a smooth rhythm is formed. Partners can assist each

other by holding the person under the arms during peer practice.

5. *African Taia-ya-taia (Tie-ya-tie)* - One partner assumes the role of a chaser. The second partner stands approximately 20 feet away. On signal, both partners balance on one foot. The chaser's goal is to tag his or her partner while maintaining a hopping position. Roles are exchanged after the first student is tagged.
6. *African Jump the Stick* - One partner grasps the two ends of a yardstick or 3-foot dowel and straightens both arms. The objective is to maintain the hold on both ends of the stick and jump through. Partners practice the skill in a stationary position, while moving forward after each jump.
7. *Alaskan Hands and Feet Race* - One partner leans forward and touches the floor. The arms and legs are straight. The objective is to jump forward while maintaining contact with the floor. The first partner performs the stunt for 10 feet or until fatigued. The second partner begins from the spot where the first partner stopped. Partners take turns advancing forward for a distance of 30 feet.
8. *English Coffee Grinder* – One partner lies on the floor on his or her right side and lifts the body so that the right arm is stiff to support the upper body. The same player raises the knees from the ground by straightening the right arm and stiffening the torso and legs. Partner Two assumes the same position except that he or she is facing Partner One. At some point, both partners begin pivoting on their supporting arm as the body creates a circle by walking on the side of the feet. Each time the partners complete one rotation, they "high five" each other with the non-supporting hand.
9. *Angola, African Jumps* - Partner One jumps ahead for distance, while Partner Two counts. The numbers in Umbunda are:

   1 = *Mosi* 2 = *Vali* 3 = *Tatu* 4 = *Kwala* 5 = *Talu*
10. *Peru, South America, Clock Skipping Game* - Two students swing a 16-foot-long rope. Other partners join a group of six to eight people and form a line behind the rope. The first set of partners run under the rope for zero, the second set jumps once, the third twice, and so on, until 12 jumps are completed. If any set of partners misses or trips the ropes, the clock must begin at zero.
11. *Chinese Rope Kicking* - Tie a long jump rope so that it is 3 to 4 feet above the ground. Partner One stands to the side of the rope and swings one leg upward to touch the rope with one foot. After both partners are successful, the rope is raised higher and the two take turns seeing how high the rope can be raised before neither one can swing one leg up and make contact with the rope.
12. *Greek Group Push-ups* - Divide the students in groups of eight (i.e., four sets of partners). Each group forms a long file line and assumes a pushup position. The first student in each line is given a tennis ball or small playground ball, which he or she rolls under students' bodies. The last person in line is standing waiting for the ball. As soon as it is retrieved, the player runs to the front of the line and rolls the ball. While the last person with the ball is running to the front, individuals in the pushup position may lower their bodies to rest.
13. *Global Count and Stretch* - One partner selects a favorite stretch or exercise such as a jumping jack or jill, sit-up, toe touch, arm circles, side stretch, or trunk twister. The second partner counts the number of exercises up to 10 from the selection of languages on page 68, and then they exchange roles.

14. *Rumanian Human Clock* - Two sets of partners (i.e., four players) form a huddle facing outward. Each player lowers the body into the push-up position. One player is facing 12 o'clock, the second player faces 3 o'clock, the third faces 6 o'clock, and the fourth is at 9 o'Clock. The feet of all four players are situated closely together and are nearly touching. On the teacher's signal, each group works together to move their bodies in a clockwise movement to complete one to four cycles of the clock.

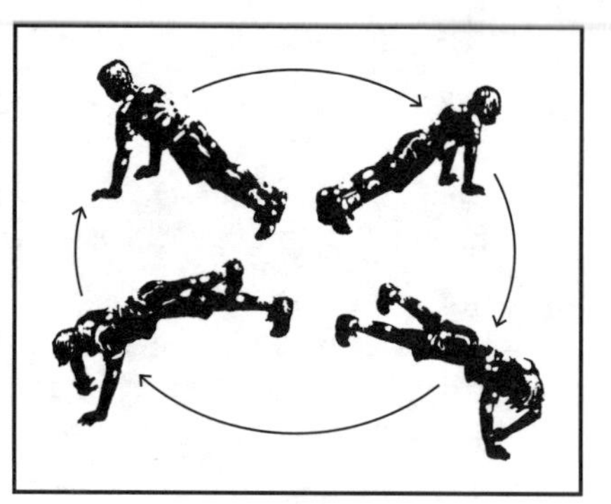

GLOBAL COUNT AND STRETCH CHART

English	French	Italian	Spanish	German
ONE	UN	UNO	UNO	EIN
TWO	DEUX	DUE	DOS	ZWEI
THREE	TROIS	TRE	TRES	DREI
FOUR	QUATRE	QUATTRO	CUATRO	VIER
FIVE	CINQ	CINQUE	CINCO	FUNF
SIX	SIX	SEI	SEIS	SECHS
SEVEN	SEPT	SETTE	SIETE	SIEBEN
EIGHT	HUIT	OTTO	OCHO	ACHT
NINE	NEUF	NOVE	NUEVE	NEUN
TEN	DIX	DIECI	DIEZ	ZEHN

CHAPTER

4

Activities for Increased Group Interaction

HUMAN STRUCTURES

OUTCOME

Reinforce the need for group efforts

DESCRIPTION OF PLAY

Found in Egypt and more commonly known as pyramids, this activity allows students to observe the physical strengths of their classmates while contributing to a common goal. Students work cooperatively to build the human structure of their choice. The word *structure* is derived from the Latin word *structura,* meaning to build.

EQUIPMENT

Gymnastics mats and human structure posters

ESSENTIAL RULES FOR PLAY

1. The human structure posters should be placed where all students can view the figures (e.g., just above eye level and taped to the wall). The students are divided into groups of 8 to 10 players.
2. Secure ample gymnastic mats to eliminate any risk of injury.
3. Groups select two to three structures and return to their mats to create a whole group structure. Structures do not need to be perfectly uniform.
4. All students should view the proper method of stepping onto a person's body by avoiding the middle of the back.
5. To avoid muscle fatigue, the completed structure should not be maintained for more than four seconds. Safety should be stressed.
6. Forum - Students should be encouraged to create or combine figures to form larger structures.
7. Whenever possible, photograph each group's completed structure.
8. Group Discussion Question - How long was the group able to hold the pose before individuals began to fatigue?

PLAYING SPACE

STRUCTURE C
Human Structures
STRUCTURE D
Human Structures
STRUCTURE E
Human Structures
STRUCTURE F
Human Structures
STRUCTURE G
Human Structures
STRUCTURE H
Human Structures
STRUCTURE I
Human Structures
STRUCTURE J
Human Structures

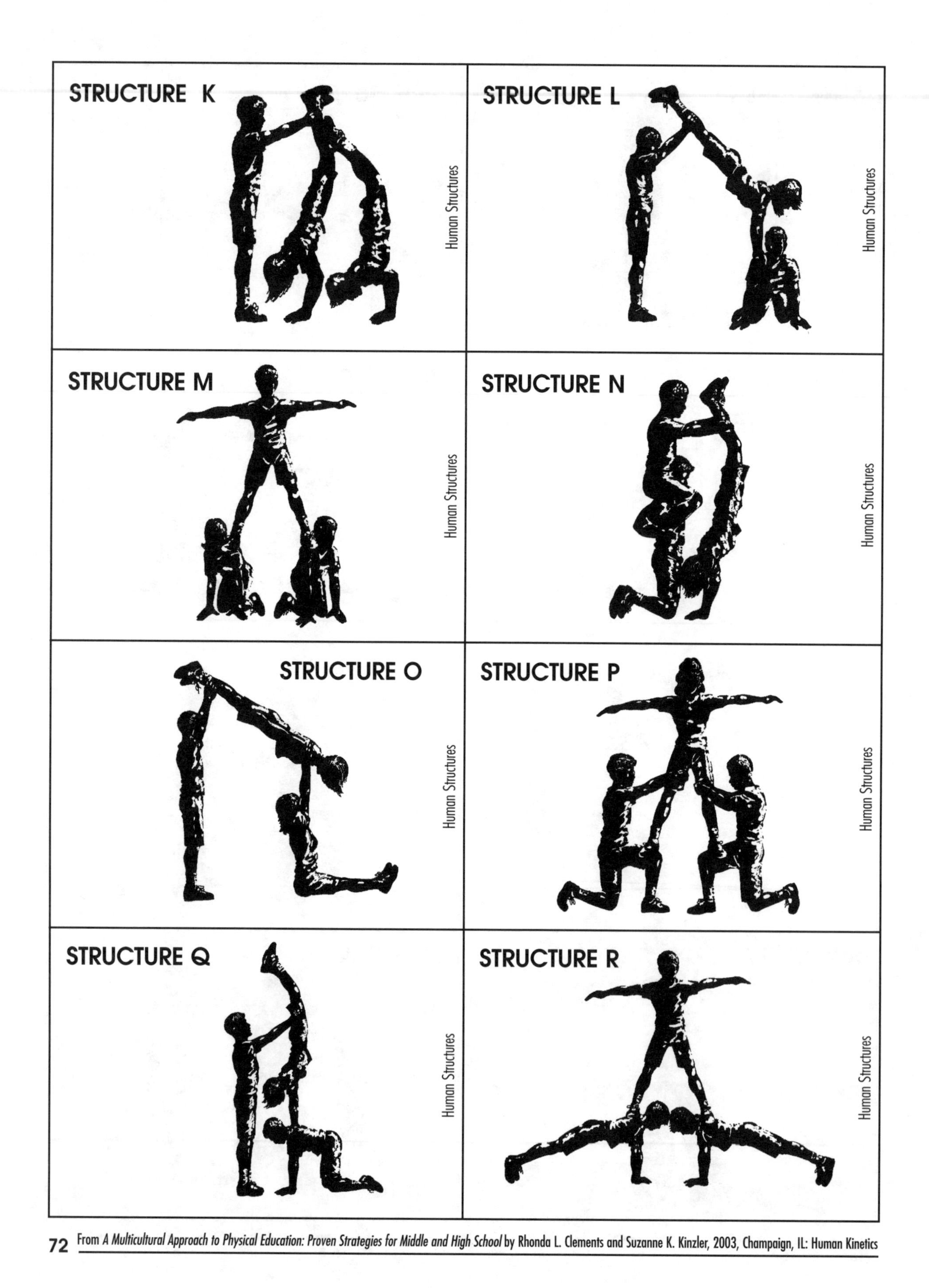
STRUCTURE K
Human Structures
STRUCTURE L
Human Structures
STRUCTURE M
Human Structures
STRUCTURE N
Human Structures
STRUCTURE O
Human Structures
STRUCTURE P
Human Structures
STRUCTURE Q
Human Structures
STRUCTURE R
Human Structures

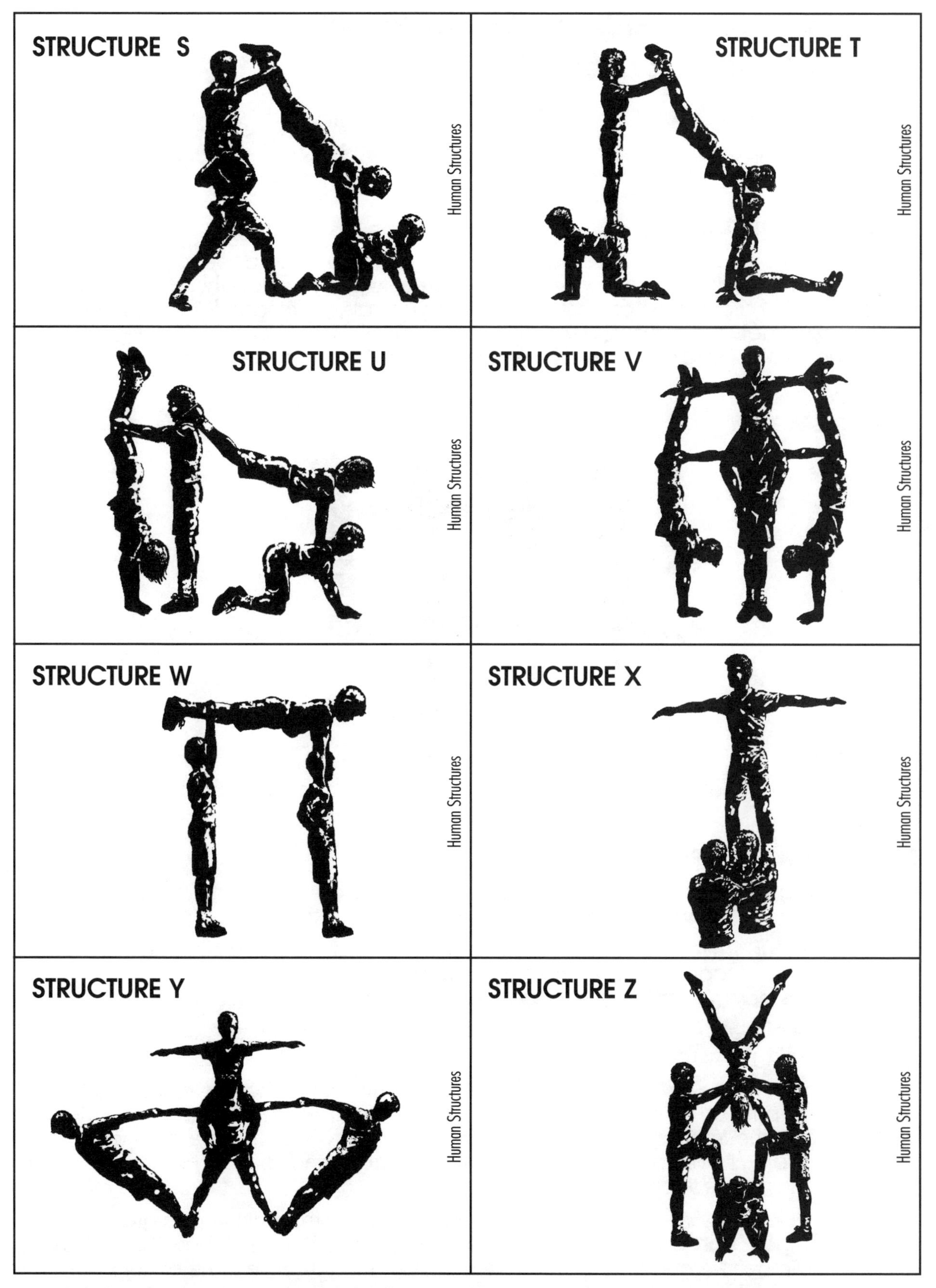
STRUCTURE S
Human Structures
STRUCTURE T
Human Structures
STRUCTURE U
Human Structures
STRUCTURE V
Human Structures
STRUCTURE W
Human Structures
STRUCTURE X
Human Structures
STRUCTURE Y
Human Structures
STRUCTURE Z
Human Structures

CULTURALLY DIVERSE COOPERATIVE ACTIVITIES

International

OUTCOME

Foster cooperation

DESCRIPTION OF PLAY

These cooperative activities are used to develop a sense of balance, agility, and physical conditioning within a supportive atmosphere. Students work within small or large groups to solve a common problem or goal. Individuals are responsible for following and giving directions, showing a sensitivity of their peer's limitations, and taking part in the group decision-making process. Elements of trust should be emphasized.

PLAYING SPACE

English Group Balance

EQUIPMENT

Planks of wood, chalk, blindfolds, soccer ball, and strips of paper

ESSENTIAL RULES FOR PLAY

1. *USA Three's Company* - Using any plank of wood, the students are challenged to maintain their balance on the object while increasing the number of participants.
2. *Italian Group Tower* - Groups of three or four students are given a piece of chalk (or a piece of tape) and are challenged to use their bodies to place a chalk mark as high as possible on the side of a wall.
3. *USA Four by Seven* - Groups of seven students are asked to move across an area of 25 feet using only four points of contact.
4. *Jamaican Hand/Foot Walk* - Groups of four players stand one player behind the other in a push up position. The last player in line maintains the position while moving forward to the front of the line. Upon moving to the front of the line, the next player at the end walks on their hands and feet to the front and so on until the line of four players has moved forward 30 feet.
5. *English Pinball Wizard* - Groups of six to eight students form a circle and grasp wrists. A fifth student stands in the middle of the circle representing a pinball. The pinball is carefully moved around the circle by leaning against the arms of his or her peers.

6. *Spanish Blindfold Soccer* - Students are divided into two groups. One half of each group is blindfolded, and the remainder of the group serve as guides. The teacher throws the soccer ball into play. Modified soccer rules apply as the guides verbally direct their partners to score a goal. Only the blindfolded students may kick the ball.
7. *Swedish Partner Sitting* - Students stand face to face and grasp wrists. Both partners assume a squatting position and lean backward so as not to lose their balance. Forum - Students explore ways to create a "group sitting stunt."
8. *Swiss Toboggan Ride* - Groups of four students are seated in a line with their legs in a V-shape. On the teacher's signal, each student lifts his or her legs slightly off the floor so that the student in front can grab the legs. The group must find the best way to move a distance of 10 feet.
9. *English Carousel* - Groups of 10 to 12 students form a circle and grasp each other's wrists. All students count off by 1s and 2s. Slowly, Group One leans backward while Group Two leans forward in a balance position.
10. *Irish Group Catch* - Three sets of partners grasp hands to form a net while one student, standing, with tightened muscles, falls slowly forward into the net of hands.
11. *Egyptian Team Tagalong* - Students are organized into groups of five or more students. The first student runs to a designated marker (a distance of 40 or more feet) and returns to the starting line. The second student in line grasps the waist of the first student. The two students run to the same designated area and return to add a third student, who grasps the waist of the second runner. Action continues until all students in the line are holding the waist of the individual in front of them.
12. *English Group Balance* - Students balance on one leg by holding the ankle of the person in front of them. Group balance is accomplished by resting the free hand on a group member's shoulder. Groups of four or five students are challenged to coordinate a hopping movement and advance forward 15 feet.
13. *Paper Tag From Sweden* - One student is given a long, thin strip of paper. This individual chases other class members, who quickly flee. When a person is tagged by the chaser, the strip of paper is torn in two halves. That person becomes another chaser who cooperates to tag other classmates. The activity continues until all but one student is in the role of chaser and is holding a piece of paper. The last person to be tagged is the winner, who initiates the second game with the new long strip of paper.
14. *Greek Tossing Circle* - Students form groups of four to six players in a circle. Each group has one tennis or small playground ball. Slowly each circle begins to move while one student throws the ball vertically in the air to be caught by the person running directly behind him or her. The goal is for each group to complete 8 to 10 revolutions without dropping the ball.
15. *Chinese Skin the Snake* - Groups of six students stand in single file, one behind the other, and bend forward, placing their right hand between the legs and grasping the left hand of the player behind his or her body. All students slowly begin walking backwards. The student in the rear lies down and the other players begin to stride over, each lying down and he or she backs over with the player's head between the legs and so on. The last player gets up first and walks forward astride the line and raises each one up after him or her until all players are in their original position.
16. *Egyptian Leap Frog (Knuzza Lawizza)* - One partner assumes a stooping position with the arms wrapped around the knees and the weight of the body supported

on the the balls of the feet with the head tucked downward. The partner takes three large steps and places both hands equally on the frog's shoulders in order to propel the body over the frog. Partners exchange roles and together complete six jumps.

17. *German Skip Stones* - Partners are challenged to move from one location of the playing area to the opposite side by using the least number of steps. Each set of partners are given six sheets of paper. One partner places the "stones" on the floor while the other steps from one stone to the other without missing. The set of partners with the least number of steps is acknowledged.
18. Group Discussion Question - Why was it so important to cooperate and assist each other in each of the activities?

OUTLANDISH ORIENTEERING

OUTCOME

Take part in group problem solving

DESCRIPTION OF PLAY

Originating in Norway, orienteering can be traced back to early civilization. When a scout or warrior went hunting, he needed to create a method to find his way home. The word *orienteering* was derived by Bjorn Kjellstrom (1910-1995), a Swedish orienteering champion who promoted the sport. Today, orienteering activities are used to acquaint students with the knowledge and skills involved with compass and basic map reading. The students move throughout a designated area and stop at numbered control points before completing a 1- to 2-mile course.

PLAYING SPACE

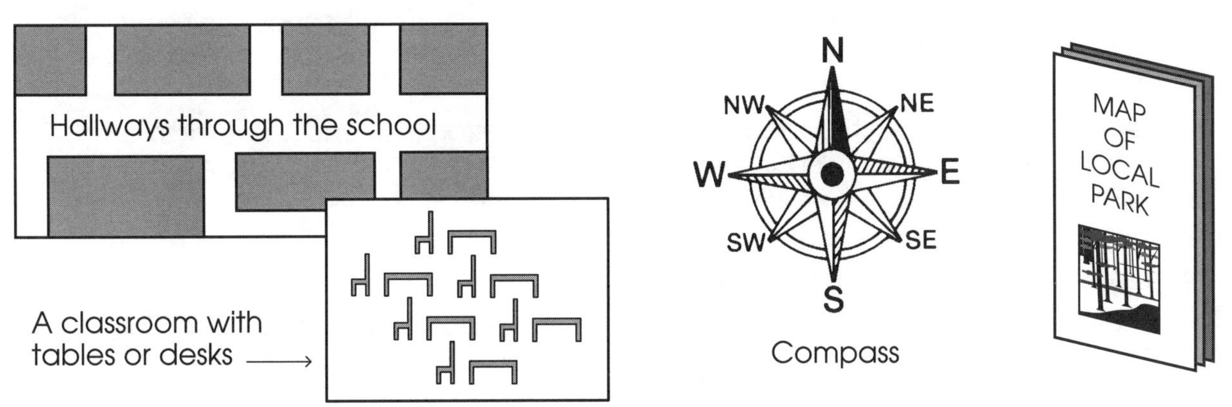

EQUIPMENT

Compasses, and map of a local park

USING A COMPASS

The four main points on a compass are North, South, East, and West. A compass needle is a tiny magnet that always points north.

a. The term *housing* refers to the degree markings on a compass (0 degrees through 360 degrees).

b. The magnetic needle North always points to the Earth's magnetic north direction.

c. The transparent bottom (with the orienteering arrow) is used to line up the magnetic north with this arrow.

d. The meridian lines are on the bottom of the compass housing. These parallel lines are lined up with lines that run north and south on a topographical map.

e. The direction line equals the bearing line equals the travel arrow. After the compass in oriented on the map, this arrow then points to the direction that the student uses to travel.

ESSENTIAL RULES FOR CLASSROOM TASKS

1. Students receive handouts identifying compass parts.
2. Students locate magnetic North and line up the orienteering arrow to the magnetic north needle. Students will then line up the travel arrow to the magnetic north direction.
3. Students locate north, south, east, and west in the classroom, and move in those directions.
4. Students locate 90 degrees, 180 degrees, 270 degrees, and 360 degrees with the travel arrow.
5. Students determine how many normal walking steps it takes to cover 25, 50, 75, and 100 feet, or how many jogging steps are required to cover the same distance.
6. While working with a partner, students will close their eyes and move to a predetermined spot in the room.

ESSENTIAL RULES FOR HALLWAY TASKS

1. Students perform compass orienteering skills throughout the school hallways. Checkpoints or control points should be placed at various locations throughout the hallways.
2. Design specific clues throughout the school. For example, one clue might read, "In the northwest science room, you might locate clue number 2." Each control point has a clue that directs the student to the next area.

ESSENTIAL RULES FOR LOCAL PARK TASKS

1. Small groups of students create a map of a local park or neighborhood. The map should indicate prominent physical features, the distance between obstacles, particular plant life, and distinguishable terrains. All maps should be compared for accuracy.
2. Using the student-designed map, each group is responsible for developing a course with 6 to 10 control points. Each control point instructs the student to perform 10 specific fitness exercises before advancing onward. Groups of students exchange maps and complete the one- to two-mile course.
3. Group Project - One group of students volunteers to develop control cards. A second group develops a course. A third group of students can position themselves to stamp a student's card as the remainder of the class completes the course. Swiftness in movement is emphasized.
4. Group Discussion Question- Did all members of the group contribute their ideas and skills while using basic orienteering skills?

HIKING FOR FITNESS

Switzerland

OUTCOME

Value nature or manmade construction

DESCRIPTION OF PLAY

The early history of the United States depended on the perseverance and physical strength demonstrated by settlers. Survival depended on their ability to understand and use the elements found in nature. Each year, from late December to April, towns and villages in the Swiss Alps fill with tourists seeking hiking experiences. Hiking For Fitness activities stress basic walking skills for nature appreciation and recreational pursuits.

PLAYING SPACE

One- to three-mile courses selected by the teacher

EQUIPMENT

Small sandwich bags to collect objects

ESSENTIAL RULES FOR PLAY

1. Forum - The students should decide upon a hiking course before leaving the school grounds. Suggestions should emphasize objects they would like to see. Examples include: plants, trees, flowers, water pathways, and wildlife animals.
2. Methods to identify directions: Students can locate the direction north by standing with their right shoulder to the sun in the morning hours, and by standing with their left shoulder to the sun in the afternoon.
3. After identifying north by the sun or using a compass, the students can identify east to the right side of the body, west to the left side of the body, and south to the rear.
4. Using the student's wrist watch to locate directions: Students having watches with numerals can hold the face of the watch in the sunlight. A toothpick or straight twig is held upright in the center of the watch. The watch is slowly turned in a circular motion until the twig's shadow falls on the hour hand. The point halfway between the number 12 and the hour hand is north. (The watch is turned clockwise in the morning hours and counterclockwise in the afternoon hours.)

5. Students can perform simple trail marking skills in wooded areas by stacking small stones or using twigs as indicators.
6. Alphabet Hike - Groups of students locate and record the objects with names that begin with each letter of the alphabet. (Example - A=Acorn)

A. ____________ H. ____________ O. ____________ V. ____________

B. ____________ I. ____________ P. ____________ W. ____________

C. ____________ J. ____________ Q. ____________ X. ____________

D. ____________ K. ____________ R. ____________ Y. ____________

E. ____________ L. ____________ S. ____________ Z. ____________

F. ____________ M. ____________ T. ____________

G. ____________ N. ____________ U. ____________

7. Scavenger Hunt - Groups of students are challenged to collect or identify objects that have the same or similar shape to that of a square, circle, diamond, triangle, heart shape, or a five-sided object.
8. Group Discussion Question - What are some of the benefits of hiking?

BEYOND THE GYMNASIUM WALLS

OUTCOME

Increase environmental awareness

DESCRIPTION OF PLAY

The following activities can be used to increase student familiarity and appreciation of the environment. Students should become aware of the need to protect and maintain the environment. The activities should demonstrate that the individual can have an immediate effect on the community's and school's well-being.

PLAYING SPACE

EQUIPMENT

Depending on the selected project, students need to be furnished with equipment for litter removal, planting, or cleaning.

ESSENTIAL RULES FOR PLAY

1. Surveying - Students work in groups of four to six and survey the local park, identifying different terrains' shrubbery and plant life on a hand-drawn map.
2. Group Task Involving a Park - Students work with a local park staff to restore a damaged area.
3. Group Task Involving The School Grounds - Groups of students are given 10 to 15 minutes to develop a school grounds improvement project. Suggestions might include (a) raking the grounds, (b) removing litter, or (c) assisting the school maintenance personnel in planting shrubbery. Whenever possible, the selected area should have a function related to athletics or physical education (e.g., grooming an athletic playing field or developing a rest area with benches).
4. Group Discussion Question - Were you pleased by the results of your improvement project?

DARING DANCE SEQUENCES

OUTCOME

Acquire aesthetic appreciation

DESCRIPTION OF PLAY

Primitive dances were used to mourn the dead, heal the sick, bring rain, or as a way to celebrate births or victory in battle. Contemporary dance styles are said to come from the pulse and heart of the people of their times. The dancer's character, personality, emotions, and movement potential emerge. The following dance-related activities encourage students to express their feelings and imaginations while reacting to a variety of music from selected eras and vocal performers.

PLAYING SPACE

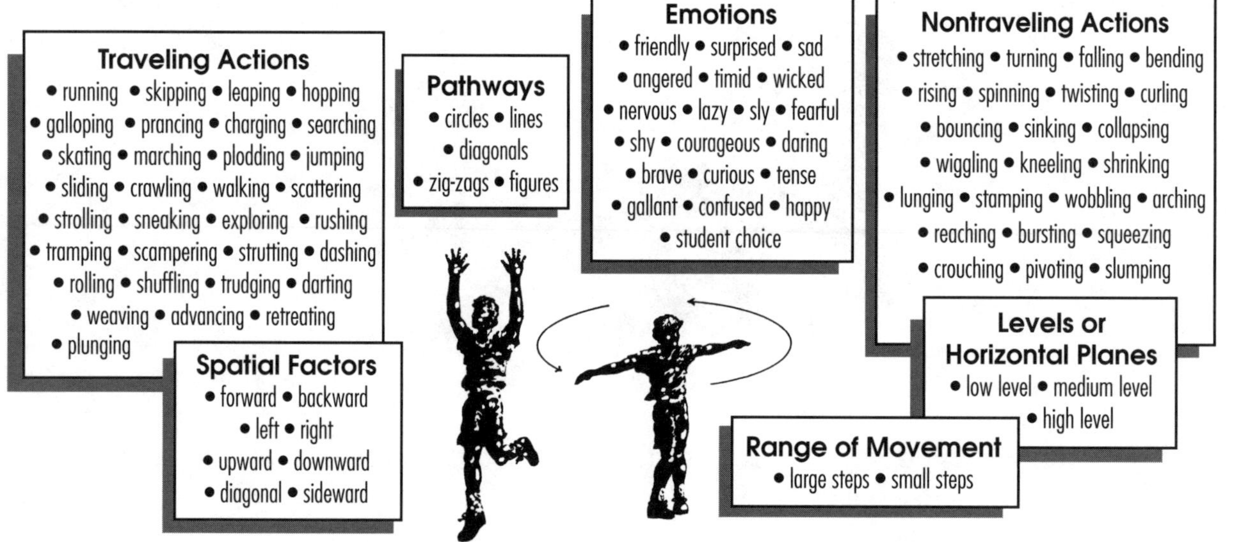

EQUIPMENT

Posters displaying dance elements, tape player, and dynamic music

ESSENTIAL RULES FOR PLAY

1. Individuals should review a variety of recorded music made available by the school library, public library, or even the teacher's personal collection. Groups of four to six students collectively choose a music selection.
2. The following dance-related factors should be posted or duplicated for all students to view:
   a. Traveling Actions - running, skipping, leaping, hopping, galloping, prancing, charging, searching, skating, marching, plodding, jumping, sliding, crawling, walking, scattering, strolling, sneaking, exploring, rushing, tramping, scampering, strutting, dashing, rolling, shuffling, trudging, darting, weaving, advancing, retreating, and plunging.

b. Nontraveling Actions - stretching, turning, falling, bending, rising, spinning, twisting, curling, bouncing, sinking, collapsing, wiggling, kneeling, shrinking, lunging, stamping, wobbling, arching, reaching, bursting, squeezing, crouching, pivoting, and slumping.
c. Spatial Factors - refers to the directions in which a person may move, such as forward, backward, left, right, upward, downward, diagonal, and sideward.
d. The Range of Movement can be changed by taking large or small steps.
e. Common floor pathways include circles, lines, diagonals, zig-zags, and figures.
f. Common levels, or horizontal planes, include low level, medium level, and high level.
g. Emotion, or moods, include using the body to show friendly, surprised, sad, angered, timid, wicked, nervous, lazy, sly, fearful, shy, courageous, daring, brave, curious, tense, gallant, confused, happy, or student choice.

3. Based on the music selection, each group is challenged to select one to three elements from each dance-related factor to form a dance sequence.
4. Forum - Students formulate a written list of the factors and practice the sequence.
5. Each group should create a 1-minute dance sequence and perform the actions to music for their peers. Select one to three elements from each dance-related factor and create a 1-minute dance sequence involving all group members.
6. Group Discussion Question - How many different traveling actions did we incorporate into our dance sequence?

In Africa, births and deaths are observed through dance. Rhythmic drumbeats are commonly used in African dance.

Irish jigs are usually performed by individuals or partners.

The Egyptian belly dance is characterized by distinct rolls of the midsection and weaving hand motions.

Tap dance originated with slaves in 19th century America who combined African rhythms with English and Irish jigs.

Many Asian dances incorporate slow, controlled hand and arm gestures.

In Spain and Mexico, men often use complicated footwork, and women express their feelings through weaving patterns of the arms.

ITALIAN FENCE (PALIFICATA)

OUTCOME

Enhance group success

DESCRIPTION OF PLAY

Soccer is the most popular sport in the world. It has been nicknamed "the people's game" worldwide. In this large group activity, forty to sixty players are actively involved using a creative rotation system designed by Italian soccer coaches.

PLAYING SPACE

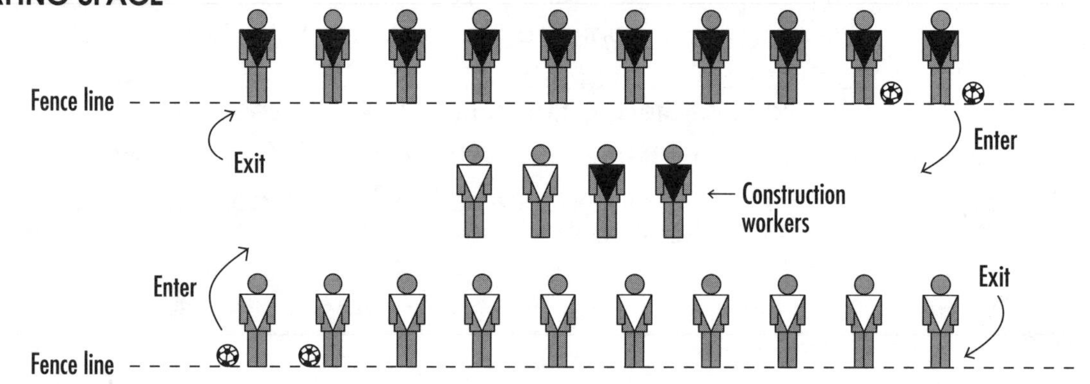

EQUIPMENT

Four to eight soccer balls

ESSENTIAL RULES FOR PLAY

1. Select three or four students to act as a group of "construction workers." Divide the remaining students into groups. Each group forms a side-by-side line on opposite sides of the playing area.
2. On the teacher's signal, the construction workers move to the center of the gymnasium. At the same time, two players from each line enter the playing area and begin dribbling the soccer ball. The construction workers try to kick the ball away from these players.
3. After a ball is kicked away by a construction worker, that player quickly returns to the end of the fence, and the line of players slides forward. The next player in line receives the kicked ball and enters the game.
4. Action continues as each player's ball is kicked, and that person quickly retreats back to the end of his or her fence line, while at the same time another player enters.
5. Play continues until all students have had an opportunity to dribble a ball. When this occurs, four new construction players can be selected.
6. Forum - Construction team discusses a strategy to maintain the fence's structure.
7. Group Discussion Question - Were there special movements that helped players to protect the soccer ball?

FOUR GOALS SOCCER

Peru

OUTCOME

Modify rules for increased participation

DESCRIPTION OF PLAY

Games resembling soccer have been played for thousands of years. The ancient Greeks kicked an inflated goatskin ball. Soldiers in ancient China played soccer as part of their army training. The first soccer shoes worn worldwide were actually boots with steel or chrome toes to prevent injury. Four Goals Soccer, common to Peru, can be played indoors when continuous action is desired.

PLAYING SPACE

EQUIPMENT

Eight cones and one to four soccer balls

ESSENTIAL RULES FOR PLAY

1. Students from the Red Group and those of the Black Group are each numbered in a consecutive order.
2. A soccer ball is placed in the middle of the playing area.
3. The teacher calls a number, for instance, "Number Two," whereby students having this number attempt to score against each other's two goals.
4. The teacher does not wait until a goal is scored to call a different number. When a new number is called, the previously called number retreats back to his or her space in line.
5. In the event that the goalie's number is called, a teammate quickly assumes the role and responsibilities. A goalie may use any body part in order to stop or pass the ball.
6. Sideline players can pass to their teammate any balls that roll to their playing space.

7. The teacher may also call two or three numbers at a time.
8. More than one soccer ball may be used.
9. At halftime, the two groups should be assigned new numbers, and the teams switch goals.
10. Forum - Group members discuss passing strategies. The students also decide to play for 8, 10, or 12 goals.
11. Group Discussion Question - Were there any group strategies that were particularly helpful in this modified version of soccer?
12. Chinese Soccer Extension - The Chinese often challenge themselves to play soccer using a small target as the goal. One variation includes placing an Indian pin inside a hula hoop at both ends of the playing area. Regular soccer rules are used with the exception of the smaller and more difficult target for each team to hit. The ball can also be shot at the pin from all directions including "behind" the circle. The task looks easy to foreign visitors but in reality, the scores are usually very low, even after a 20-minute non-stop playing session.

CHICAGO SOFTBALL

OUTCOME

Conform to group needs

DESCRIPTION OF PLAY

The game of 16-inch Softball originated in Chicago in 1887, by a man named George W. Hancock, as an indoor version of baseball. Back then, a 17-inch ball was used to play the game. The game grew in popularity during the depression era of the 1930s when gloves were considered a luxury. The game remains very popular today in the midwestern area of the United States due to its lack of required equipment and the increased success level.

PLAYING SPACE

16" Softball

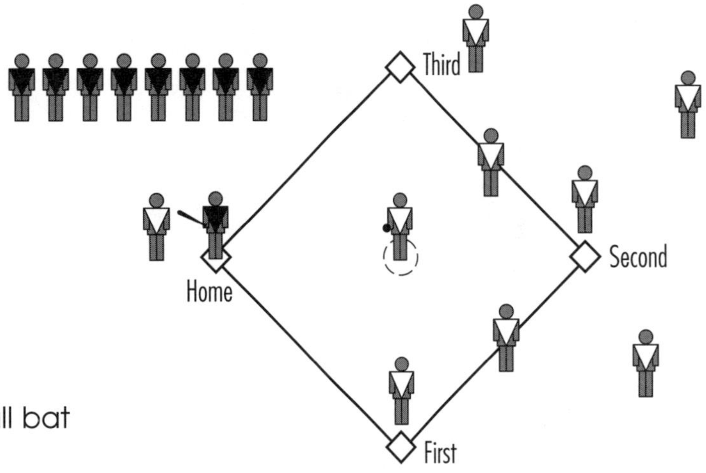

Third

Second

Home

First

EQUIPMENT

Several 16-inch softballs and a softball bat

ESSENTIAL RULES FOR PLAY

1. The students are divided into two teams. Gloves are not required, although it is advisable for the catcher to wear a glove, chest protector, and face mask.
2. Students use the Sukatan, or sandlot, method from the Philippines, of deciding which team goes first by allowing one player from each team to wrap hands around the bat. Fists must touch each other on the bat. The hands climb quickly to the top until the last hand places his or her thumb on the top of the bat.
3. Pitching - The pitcher must begin with one or both feet on the mound. The pivot foot must remain in contact with the plate until the ball leaves the hand. Slow pitch rules (i.e., an arch of 3 feet) apply. A fast pitch is called a ball.
4. A batter receives a walk on four balls, but can strike out by hitting a foul ball with a two-strike count.
5. Runners may attempt to steal bases.
6. All other slow pitch rules can be applied.
7. Forum - Students are encouraged to make use of place-hitting strategies.
8. The official 16-inch Clincher™ is manufactured and patented by J. DeBeer and Son, Inc.
9. Group Discussion Question - What are the advantages to playing with a larger softball?

THREE TEAM SOFTBALL

OUTCOME

Reflect upon the importance of collaboration

DESCRIPTION OF PLAY

Softball was intended as a winter substitute for baseball. In 1908, the National Amateur Playground Ball Association was formed and promoted the idea of playing the game outdoors. This activity eliminates the situation where one team is left losing. It also increases the likelihood that more students will have turns at bat before three outs occur. The English word *team* stems from the Latin word, *ducere* meaning to pull together.

PLAYING SPACE

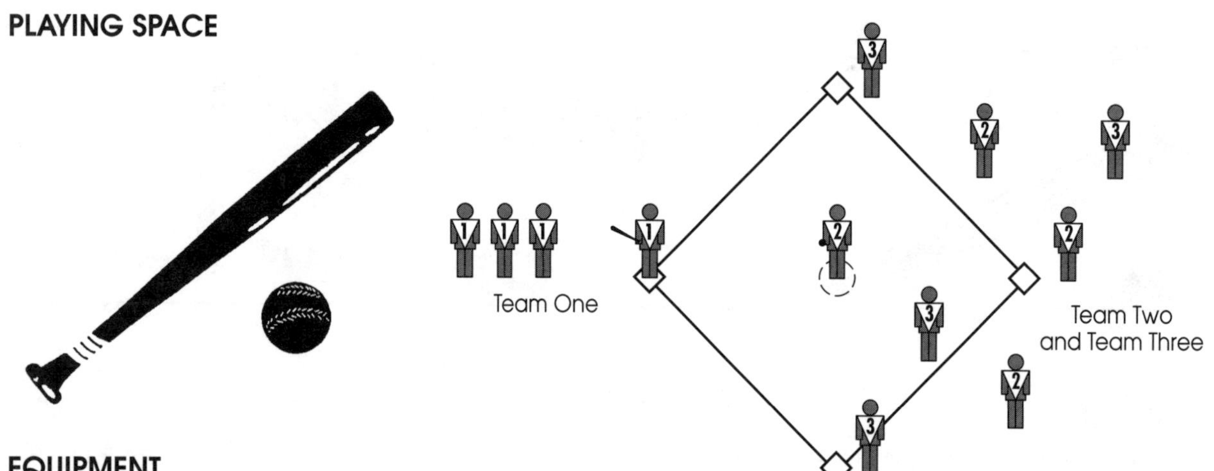

EQUIPMENT

Several 16-inch softballs and a softball bat

ESSENTIAL RULES FOR PLAY

1. Divide the students into three groups or teams (i.e., Team One, Team Two, and Team Three).
2. Team Two and Team Three work together performing fielding positions while Team One performs batting skills.
3. After Team One has either made three outs or every student on the team has had a turn at bat, Team Two is given an opportunity to bat, followed by Team Three.
4. Forum - Groups in the field reposition players for effective defense.
5. General softball rules apply.
6. Group Discussion Question - Were we able to work collaboratively with each team while in the field?

COLLECTIVE SOFTBALL

OUTCOME

Create opportunities for success

DESCRIPTION OF PLAY

Early names for softball include "kittenball," "mush-ball," "army ball," and "recreation ball." In 1933, "softball" became the official name under the auspice of the Amateur Softball Association of America. Collective Softball increases opportunities for the individual student to find success in obtaining points for his or her team.

PLAYING SPACE

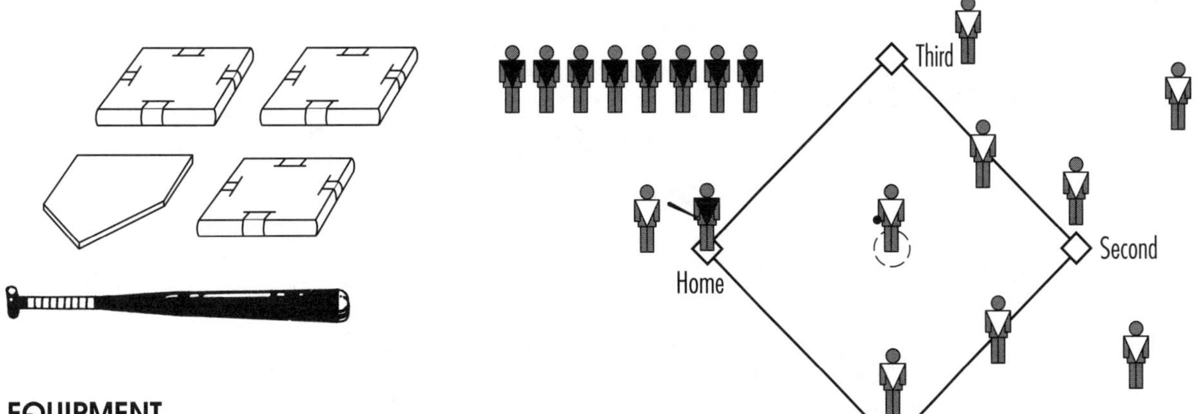

EQUIPMENT

Four bases, softball bat, and balls

ESSENTIAL RULES FOR PLAY

1. Divide the students into two teams. All students assume typical softball playing positions.
2. Students score points by hitting the softball and attempting to make contact with all four bases without being put out.
3. The batter scores one point for every base obtained. For example, if a batter passes first base and is put out at second base, he or she scores one point for having reached first base. Hence, a home run equals four points.
4. Forum - Teams prepare and submit a list of the batting order.
5. All other softball rules apply.
6. Group Discussion Question - How important was it to organize the batting order to increase the opportunities for success?
7. Extension – In "Hey, Batter, Batter," only four batters may face the pitcher in an inning. Hence, the inning is over when three players are out, or when the fourth batter scores, is forced out, or is put out by the ball reaching any base ahead of him or her. This rule greatly encourages the students to display additional effort.

FINNISH BASEBALL (PESAPALLO)

Finland

OUTCOME

Engage in new playing skills

DESCRIPTION OF PLAY

Lauri "Wheatstone" Pihkale introduced Finland to *Pesapallo* (Finnish for baseball) in 1922 after returning from a visit to the USA. Finland's schoolchildren play the game as part of their school curriculum and more than 700,000 spectators watch Finnish National Baseball games. Using rules similar to baseball, students bat a vertically pitched ball to score runs.

PLAYING SPACE

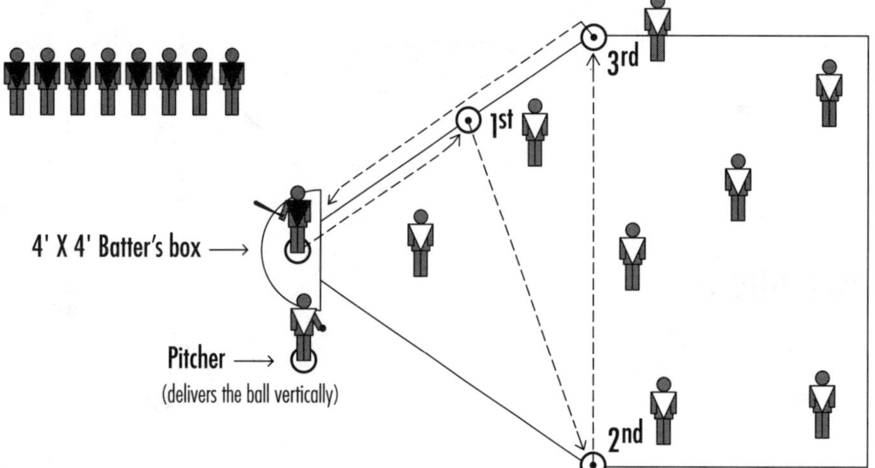

EQUIPMENT

Bases, softball, and one fungo bat

ESSENTIALS RULES FOR PLAY

1. Students are divided into two teams of nine players each. Action begins with a player from each team performing the "hand over hand method," grasping the bat to determine which team bats first.
2. The batter stands in a 4- by 4-foot batter's box. The pitcher stands to the right and away from the batter and tosses the ball (underhand toss) upward 4 to 6 feet. The batter must hit the ball on the descent.
3. Upon a successful hit, the batter then runs into the field to the left to first base and then proceeds to second, third, and home.
4. The batter has three strikes when at bat. He or she is given a base on balls when two pitches do not fall within the batter's box.
5. The batter is out if a fly ball is caught, which is called a "fly hit," or a ball is fielded to the base ahead of the runner.

6. A base runner may also be tagged or forced out at a base.
7. Each team is given three outs and nine innings.
8. Forum - Students react and take steps to re-position their players in the outfield to accommodate the large fielding area.
9. Group Discussion Question - How difficult was it to run in an unfamiliar pathway after you hit the ball?

U.S. Baseball	Pesapallo
Three bases	Three bases
Homeplate diamond	Homeplate round
Three strikes	Three strikes
Three outs	Three outs
Run in a diamond pathway	First base is in the same direction as third base
Pitching in a line	Vertical pitching (3-feet over the batter's head)
Swing anytime	Swing when ball moves downward
"Throwing a player out"	"Wounding"
Can be a slow game	Faster tempo of play
Nine innings	Nine innings

PLAY BALL!

READY OR NOT RING HOCKEY

France

OUTCOME

Adhere to rules

DESCRIPTION OF PLAY

The concept of hockey can be traced back to Persia, more than 2000 years B.C. The French word *hoquet* refers to the curved staff of a shepherd's crook. The early balls in the 1800s were made of rubber. These objects were cut with small angles so they would bounce unevenly. Oak sticks with lead inserted at the far tip gave the player additional driving power. Modern field hockey is based on hurling, bandy, and shinty played in the British Isles and China. In Ready or Not Ring Hockey, the student places the stick tip inside the donut-like puck while moving, passing, driving, or shooting at a goal.

PLAYING SPACE

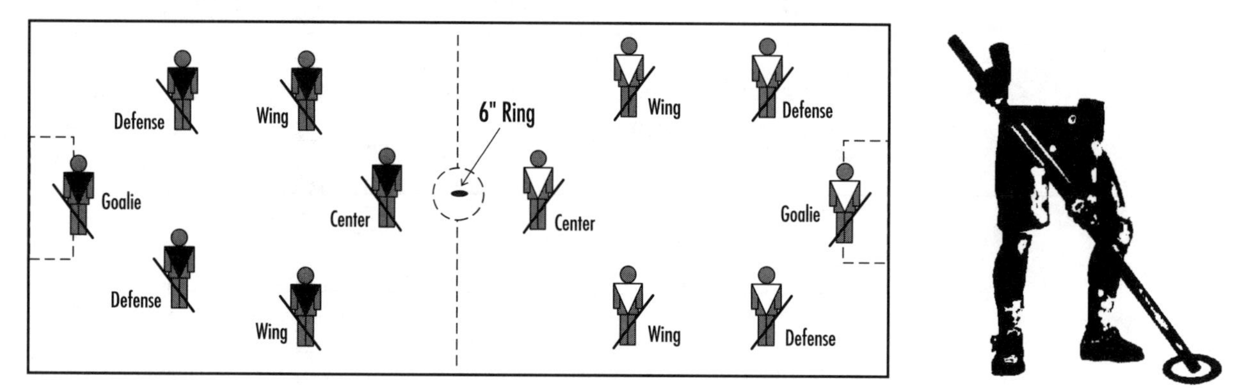

EQUIPMENT

Ring Hockey sticks or 4-foot wooden dowels with a taped stripe to identify the two different teams, and one 6-inch ring

ESSENTIAL RULES FOR PLAY

1. Each team consists of one goalie, one center, two wings, and two defensive players.
2. Begin the game with a face-off (a dropped ring between the two center players).
3. The ring must remain on the floor. The ring cannot be slapped, kicked, or pushed by any object other than the stick.
4. Wing players may travel up and down the sides of the playing area.
5. Defensive players may not cross the center line.
6. Out of Play - If possible, there should not be an out of bounds. If the ring does go out of an agreed area, the last team to have contact loses possession. In this case, play is initiated at the point it went out of bounds.
7. A team is awarded one point for every goal scored beyond the net or cones.
8. A face-off occurs after every goal.

9. Penalty Shots - One free shot with only the goalie on defense is made for the following:

   - Kneeing
   - Slashing
   - Throwing the stick
   - Holding
   - Hooking
   - Elbowing
   - Tripping
   - Interference

   All penalty shots are taken from 25 feet in front of the goal.
10. Six new players enter the game and replace their teammates each time a goal is scored.
11. Forum - Groups are responsible for determining their team's playing positions and strategies.
12. Group Discussion Question - Did individuals adhere to the rules and remain in their playing spaces?

AFRICAN BOLO BALL

OUTCOME

Adapt to physical limitations

DESCRIPTION OF PLAY

Students advance a basketball down a court by raising only one hand to pass and catch between teammates in order to score a goal. It is not uncommon to play this game on hard dirt surfaces in Africa.

PLAYING SPACE

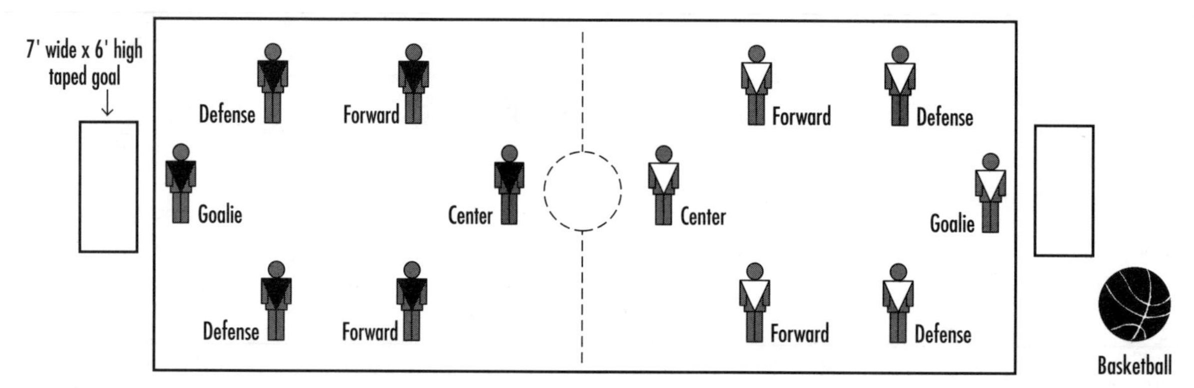

EQUIPMENT

One basketball and two taped goals

ESSENTIAL RULES FOR PLAY

1. A rectangle goal that is 7 feet wide and 6 feet high is taped on each wall at opposite ends of the playing area. The students are organized in groups of six. Each group is composed of one center, two forwards, two defense players, and one goal keeper.
2. Play begins when the teacher bounces a basketball on the floor in the center of the mid-circle. The ball should not bounce higher than each center player's chest level, and each center can try to snatch the ball as soon as it reaches their waist level.
3. Players advance the ball by using an overhand tap, by smashing it downward, by a slooping throw off the floor, or by bouncing the ball off an upper body part or any of the gymnasium's four walls. Players may also dribble the ball, as in basketball for three bounces.
4. A foul is awarded if the ball is kicked, and the opposite team receives possession.
5. The goalie is the only player to use both hands to block a ball. He or she may also score a goal by throwing the ball to a forward, who attempts to score. Only one hand is permitted in the throwing action.
6. The object is to be the first group to score 10 points. The ball is bounced in the center of the mid-circle by the teacher after each score.
7. Forum - Students discuss the best means to advance the ball.
8. Group Discussion Question - How important was it to use different body parts to advance the ball when only using one hand?

SWEEP ME AWAY BROOM BALL

Canada

OUTCOME

Analyze different playing positions

DESCRIPTION OF PLAY

Popular in Canada, Broom Ball is a high-scoring, quick action game commonly played outside during cold winter months or in a limited space during all types of weather. Students use sawed off brooms to sweep an eraser, a puck, or a ball through the opposite team goal.

PLAYING SPACE

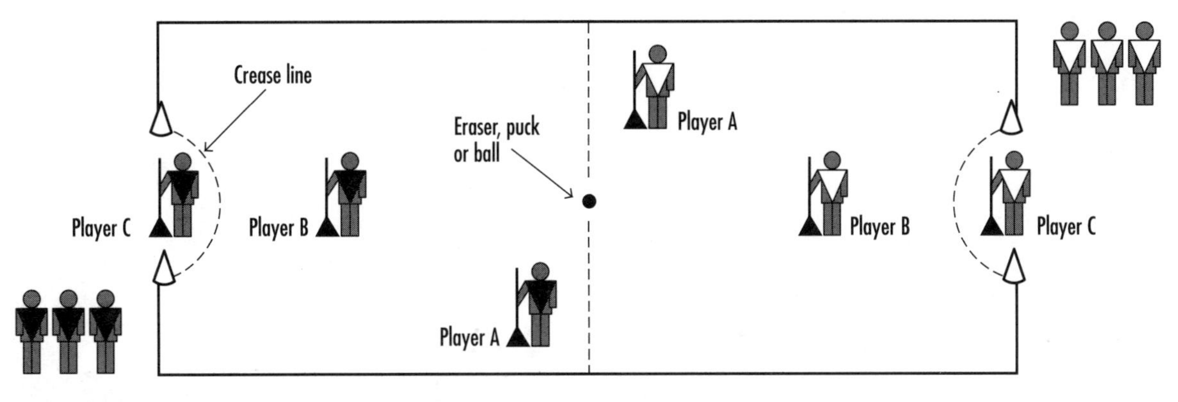

EQUIPMENT

Six brooms and a foam soccer ball, classroom eraser, or hockey puck

ESSENTIAL RULES FOR PLAY

1. There are only three designated playing positions in Sweep Me Away Broom Ball. Player A takes the broom on the right side of the center court. Player B takes the broom at the right side of each team's midcourt. Player C assumes the role in the goal area.
2. Play begins with both teams' brooms placed on the floor in the suggested playing positions. The ball rests in the middle of the playing facility. On the teacher's signal, all students pick up their brooms and begin to play.
3. The broom heads may not be lifted more than 2 feet off the floor.
4. Two hands are used to hold the broom at all times. All shots are two-handed. One-handed, uncontrolled swings are not permitted.
5. The puck or ball may be swept, tapped, pushed, or hit in a driving motion, but may not be dragged along the floor by the broom head.
6. The three players continue to play until a goal is scored. After each goal, play is stopped and a student from both teams substitutes into Player A's position. Player A then moves to the B position, and Player B takes Player C's position. Player C moves

to the end of his or her teammate's sideline. Hence, each student is given the opportunity to perform each position as a natural form of rotation.

7. No body part may be used to stop the puck or ball.
8. A crease line should be taped or marked 4 feet in front of the goal. Offensive players are not permitted to touch the ball beyond this line or enter this area. This is a safety precaution to protect the goalie.
9. Forum - Students engage in a discussion concerning offensive strategies.
10. Group Discussion Question - Was there a particular playing position that received more of the action?

EGYPTIAN GROUP BOWLING

OUTCOME

Interpret results for group efforts

DESCRIPTION OF PLAY

Games related to bowling can be traced back to 5200 B.C. Egypt, where archaeologists found stone balls and nine pins in a child's tomb. The Dutch brought bowling to America in the 1660s. America's first indoor bowling alley opened in 1840 in Manhattan, New York. Paeng Nepomuceno was born in the Philippines in 1957, and is acknowledged worldwide as the greatest international bowler in the history of the sport. Egyptian Group Bowling is played with a large number of students who score points collectively.

PLAYING AREA

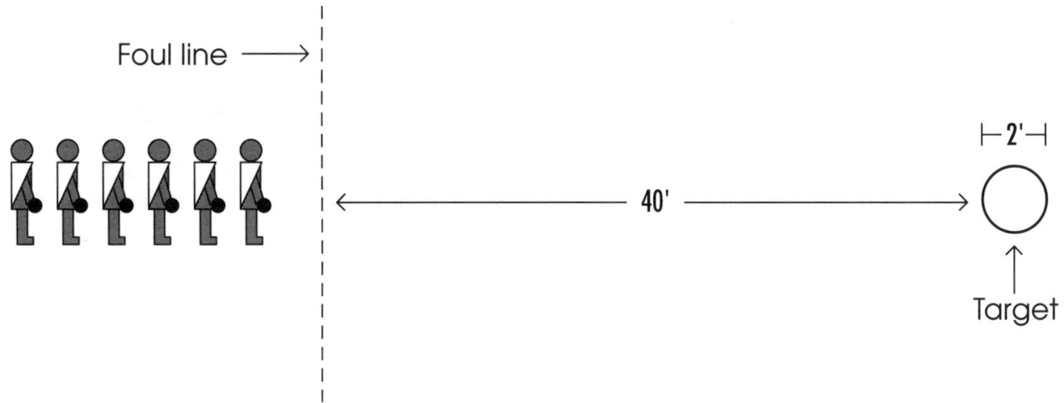

EQUIPMENT

Softballs, tennis balls, or croquet balls

ESSENTIAL RULES FOR PLAY

1. Groups of six to eight students measure a playing area of 40 or more feet. A foul line is drawn at one end of the playing field, and a 2-foot circle at the end of the playing field.
2. Individual students take turns bowling a softball or tennis ball at the target.
3. After each student has bowled his or her ball, the score is tallied according to the number of participating students in the line. If there are six students in the line participating, for example, the student bowling nearest the center of the target earns six points. The next scores five points and so on.
4. Students agree to play for 50, 70, or 100 points.
5. Group Discussion Question - Did individuals demonstrate a positive attitude even when their score was lower or higher than others in the game?

PIGSKIN PASS

OUTCOME
Practice patience

DESCRIPTION OF PLAY
In Chaucer's time (1343-1400), the ball was usually made from the inflated bladder of a pig, hence its acquired nickname, "pigskin." In 1906, the forward pass became legal. In this activity, individual students from two opposing groups tag as many opponents as possible while having possession of their group's football.

PLAYING SPACE

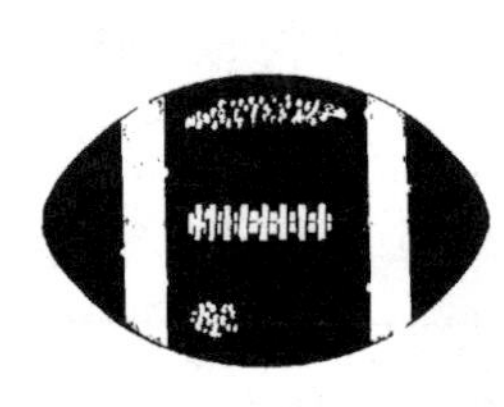

EQUIPMENT
Colored jerseys and two footballs

ESSENTIAL RULES FOR PLAY
1. The students are divided into two groups. Each group is identified by wearing different colored jerseys, pinnies, or flags, and each group has one football.
2. Students position themselves randomly throughout the playing area.
3. On the teacher's signal, each team passes their football using any throwing skill.
4. When a student receives a pass, he or she is eligible to tag a student on the opposite team.
5. When a student is tagged he or she becomes a member of the opposing group, and immediately wears the opposite team's playing color.
6. Play continues until all students from one group have been tagged.
7. Forum - Students are encouraged to utilize a variety of dodging and darting techniques to avoid being tagged.
8. Group Discussion Question - Was speed as important as accuracy in this game?

SIX MINUTE TOUCHDOWN

OUTCOME

Promote teamwork

DESCRIPTION OF PLAY

In 1882, Walter Camp from Yale University created rules for American football that included downs. That is, a team had three chances to go five yards, or the ball had to be given to the opponent at the spot the person carrying the ball was brought down. He also designated a quarterback to set the plays. In 1934 Stephen Elper of Hebron, Nebraska, created six-man football to decrease injuries and designed a new game appropriate for grammar- through high-school children. Six Minute Touchdown can be played in a gymnasium of limited space by using a foam or lightweight football and teams of six players.

PLAYING SPACE

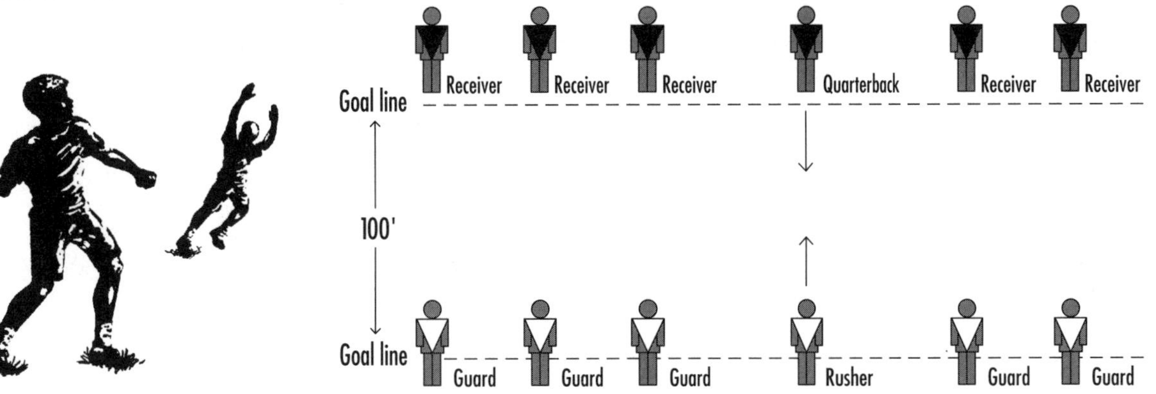

EQUIPMENT

Colored jerseys and one football

ESSENTIAL RULES FOR PLAY

1. The students are divided into groups of six players. Two groups play at one end of the field and two groups play facing the opposite end of the field if space is available. Teams are given possession of the ball 5 yards from the goal line.
2. One student is designated the quarterback and the other five players are eligible receivers. On the defense team, one player is a designated rusher and the other five players guard the receivers.
3. The team with possession (offense) has three trials (downs) to advance the ball over their opponent's (defense) goal line. If the offense fails to score a touchdown (six points), the defensive team takes possession of the ball 5 yards from the goal line.
4. The rusher may cross the line of scrimmage only after he or she has slowly counted out loud for 5 seconds.

5. The ball is dead when the offensive player has been tagged below the head by a defender.
6. The ball is advanced by the forward pass.
7. Groups play for 6 minutes, or they may agree to play for a specified total of points.
8. Forum - Individuals are encouraged to play different positions within their group and to reinforce the primary responsibility of each playing position.
9. Group Discussion Question - Did it help to switch playing positions during the 6-minute time period so that all players had a specific role?

TRY HARDER HANDBALL

OUTCOME

Negotiate playing positions

DESCRIPTION OF PLAY

Team Handball was first called European Handball, and was played with 11 players on a team in Scandinavian countries in the early 1900s. Alexander the Great (356-323 B.C.) played handball on what the Greeks called a *sphairisterion*, or ball court. It was first played outdoors and then became an indoor sport with seven players in 1920. *Yemari* means handball in Japan. This modified indoor handball activity combines the skills of basketball dribbling and passing with the scoring techniques common to soccer.

PLAYING SPACE

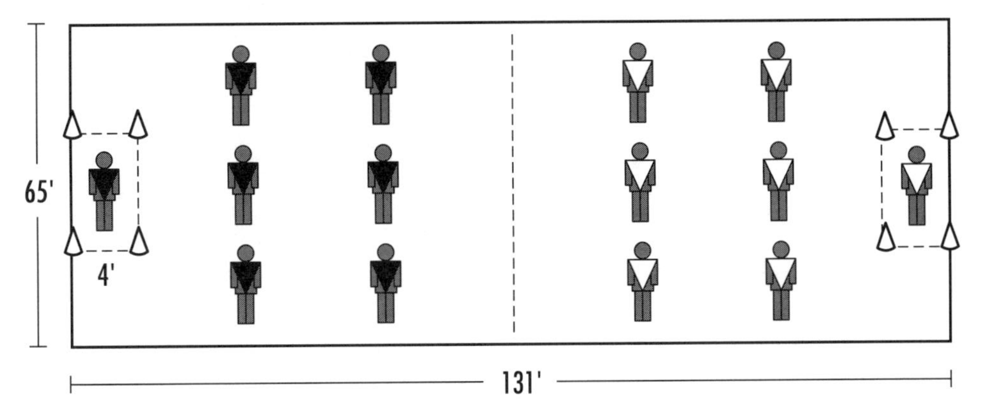

EQUIPMENT

Jerseys to distinguish teams, eight cones for goals, and one foam soccer ball

ESSENTIAL RULES FOR PLAY

1. Students are divided into two teams. Each team has seven players on the field at one time. This includes the offense, defense, and the goalie.
2. Forum - Each team decides how many players will play offense and how many are needed to play defense positions.
3. Play begins with a throw-off taken by one team at the center of the playing area. The student has 3 seconds to throw a 7-inch ball.
4. The players attempt to throw the ball into the opponents' goal in order to score one point.
5. The players must complete three passes for the goal to count.
6. Players must stay out of their opponents' goalie box in order for a goal to count. Players are allowed in their own goalie box.
7. Each player has 5 seconds and/or three steps before a pass or shot attempt must be made. A student may catch, throw, bounce, or strike the ball in any manner

using any body part that is above the knee. When using a bounce method, or dribble, the student may stop, dribble with one hand, and then take three additional steps.

8. Students defend their goal by using defensive skills common to basketball. The goalie may use any body part to prevent the ball from scoring.
9. Unnecessary roughness will result in a change of possession and/or a penalty shot, depending on the nature of the foul.
10. After each goal, a throw-off is taken at the center line by the team that did not score.
11. Group Discussion Question - How important was it to reposition players so that maximum success was likely?

CHECKMATE HANDBALL

China

OUTCOME

Maintain a high level of motivation

DESCRIPTION OF PLAY

The game Chess was created more than 4,000 years ago by the Chinese as a way to imagine creative strategies in warfare. In this activity, students are assigned positions similar to those in chess. Teams advance the ball by converting a kicked or dribbled ball to an air ball that is then thrown to the designated King or Queen to score one point.

PLAYING SPACE

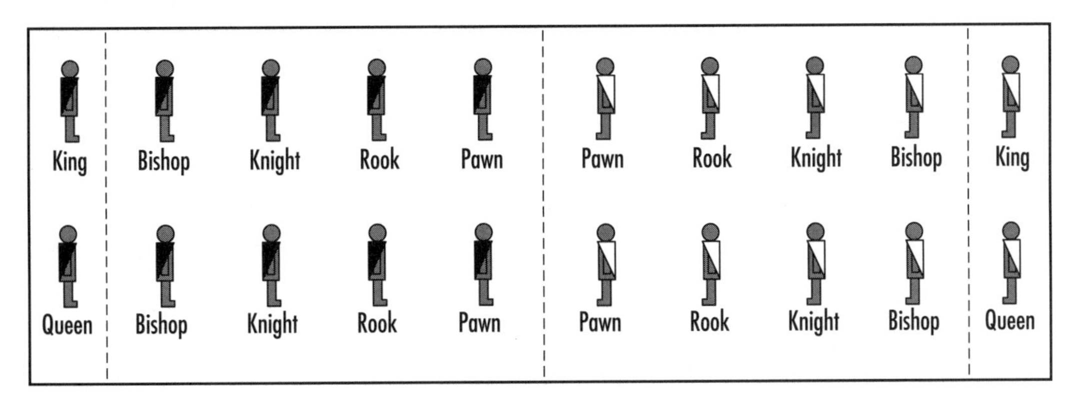

EQUIPMENT

One foam soccer ball

ESSENTIAL RULES FOR PLAY

1. Each team consists of two Rooks, two Bishops, two Pawns, two Knights, one Queen, and one King.
2. Play begins with a jump ball between opposing Pawns. If a ball is caught from the jump by a teammate, players immediately begin passing the ball in an attempt to throw the ball to a King or Queen, who are positioned behind the goal.
3. With the exception of the King or Queen, who are always playing offense, all players play both offense and defense depending on if their team has possession of the ball.
4. The ball may be advanced using the soccer dribble, or it may be converted to an air ball so that it may be thrown from player to player. This action is possible by trapping the ball between the ankles and jumping while lifting the ball to the hands. Air balls are also possible by kicking the ball into the air into the hands of a teammate or by kicking the ball and having it rebound off a wall into the hands of a teammate.
5. A ball that crosses the goal line (the entire end line of a gymnasium at either end)

from a foot dribble does not score a point. The ball must be converted to an air ball and thrown to the King or Queen. Any ball rolling across the goal line is kicked back into the playing field of play, where it is converted to an air ball and passed to the King or Queen.

6. Students guard a player who has possession of the ball by using the same defensive techniques that are used in basketball.
7. A jump ball is taken after each successful score, or in the event that two opposing players gain possession of an air ball at the same time.
8. Forum - Students use a clipboard and paper to illustrate a sequence of passes to score a point.
9. Substitutions are called after each score.
10. Group Discussion Question - What elements of strategy were obvious in both groups' offensive play?

UNLIMITED PASS VOLLEYBALL

OUTCOME

Become empowered

DESCRIPTION OF PLAY

In 1895, William Morgan of Holyoke, Massachusetts, used a bladder of a basketball and a tennis net strung between two wooden posts to create the game of volleyball. The original game contained innings, outs, and nine players on a team. The rules in Unlimited Pass Volleyball are very similar to William Morgan's concept of unlimited hits. Each team is allowed an unlimited number of passes on their side in order to return the ball to the opposite team's side. Cooperation is emphasized.

PLAYING SPACE

EQUIPMENT

One volleyball and a 6-foot net

ESSENTIAL RULES FOR PLAY

1. The class is divided into two teams of six players each. A rope or net is raised to 6 or 7 feet at its highest point.
2. A student has the choice of using any serving technique. The server may also use the overhead pass or the forearm technique to a teammate on his or her own side of the court, who may assist in the serve. The server begins play in the right hand corner behind the baseline.
3. A ball must go over the net without touching it and land within the boundaries of the opponent's court in order to be considered a legal serve.
4. Each team is allowed unlimited passes on its own side in order to return the ball to the opposing team's side.
5. A team may score points only when it has the serve. Whenever a team wins the serve from the opponent, its members rotate before the serve by moving in a clockwise direction. That is, the front line of three players moves from left to right and the back line moves right to left.

6. Groups decide to play for either 15 points or for 15-minute halts.
7. Forum - Students compare the value of returning the ball immediately or using an unlimited number of times to set the ball in an effort to spike it strategically into the opposing team's court.
8. Group Discussion Question - How did the unlimited pass rule increase opportunities for strategies among teammates?
9. Extension - *European Volleyball* - In Europe, many physical educators use the same basic court set-up as in American volleyball, but substitute the USA ball with an inflatable rubber ball that weighs 2.2 lbs. or 1kg to increase the fitness level of their students. They also use a standard medicine ball when the 2.2-lb. rubber ball is not available. Play begins with the ball being tossed underhand over the net from behind the half-line by the server. The ball must be caught and then tossed underhand to two other players on one's team before being tossed back over the net. All players must remain alert and one point is scored when the ball is missed or dropped and hits the ground. Play continues for 15 points. All other regular volleyball rules apply.

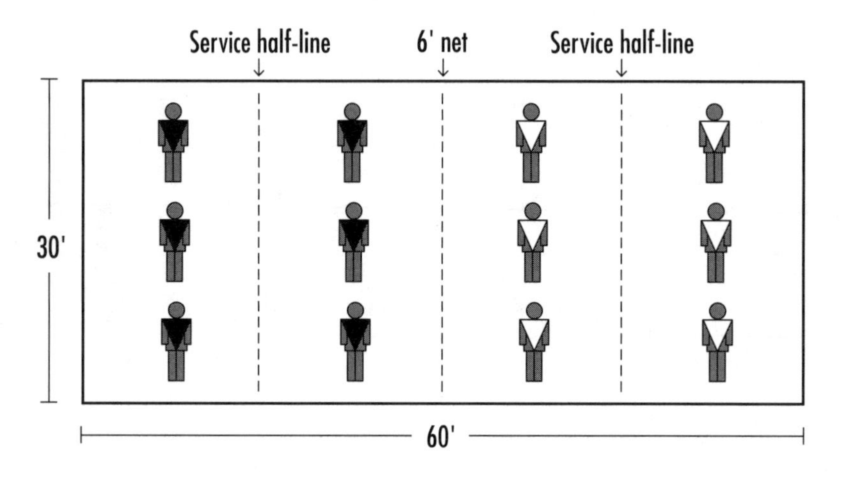

FANTASTIC FISTBALL

OUTCOME

Verbalize strategies

DESCRIPTION OF PLAY

Fistball stems from Germany where it was called *faustball.* The German word *faust* means fist. The International Fistball Association plays with a Drohnn Ball measuring 26 inches in circumference. Teams utilize only five players and contemporary rules reflect the sport of volleyball. The objective of this early USA version is to volley and rally a large ball over a net using a striking movement.

PLAYING SPACE

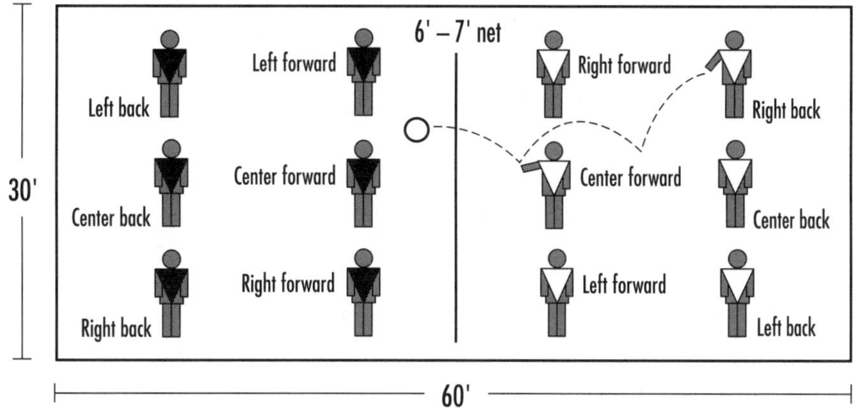

EQUIPMENT

60-inch cageball or 15-inch floater volleyball, and a 6- to 7-foot net

ESSENTIAL RULES FOR PLAY

1. The game consists of six students on each team, although larger teams can be successful. The net should be between 6 and 7 feet high to encourage active participation from all players. The contemporary 15-inch floater volleyball can be used if the traditional 60-inch cageball is not available.
2. The game begins with the right back line player bouncing the ball in such a way that a forward player can strike the ball with his or her fist over the net. Back line players are encouraged to communicate with front line players throughout this action.
3. If the forward line player fails to serve the ball over the net, the action is called a "side out" and the opposing team receives the serve.
4. After the ball has been served, the opposing team attempts to return the ball over the net. One bounce is allowed before the ball must be returned over the net. Each forward has an opportunity for service, when his or her team gains service.
5. The forward line players and the back line players change positions after their team has scored 5 points.

6. The ball may only be struck with the fist three times and allowed to bounce once before being returned to the challenging team.
7. Balls falling or bouncing on the boundary line are considered in play.
8. Balls served over the net may be played before the ball drops and bounces.
9. The defensive team may try to block the ball when the offensive team is serving. Defensive players may not, however, reach over the net or come in contact with the net in attempting to block.
10. Forum - Teams agree to play to 15 or 20 points; they also discuss ways to perform the best service techniques.
11. Extension - Monster Fist Ball allows 15 or more students per team to play on an over-size court. A 3- to 4-foot beach ball or recreational plastic ball is used.
12. Group Discussion Question - Which techniques were most effective when trying to return the ball?

STICKBALL

OUTCOME
Compare methods of skill execution

DESCRIPTION OF PLAY
Originating in England during the 18th century, the game of stickball allows the ball to be batted after being tossed up in their air and hit by the student (i.e., self-hitting or fungo hitting); it may be pitched so that it bounces once before reaching the batter; or the student may request an underhand or overhand pitch to increase the opportunities for success.

PLAYING SPACE

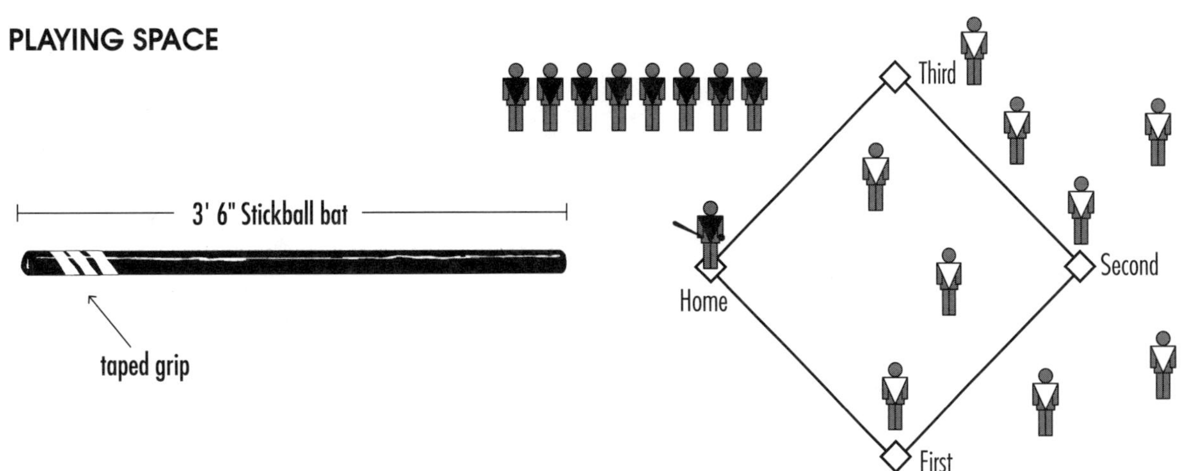

EQUIPMENT
A stickball bat, pink spaldeens or tennis balls

ESSENTIAL RULES FOR PLAY
1. Play begins with the class divided into two teams. The first, second, third, and home plates may be designated with chalk, regulation softball bags, or common objects, such as the markings on a side of a building or gymnasium cones.
2. Pink Spaldeens or tennis balls are most commonly used. Balls may also be cut in half when the playing area is limited.
3. The game begins with a student from each team following the old custom of alternating "hand over hand" grasping of the stickball bat. When the top of the bat is reached, the student whose hand is nearest to the top has the choice of having his or her team either bat or take the field.
4. Students assume playing positions as in softball or baseball.
5. Individuals at bat decide to fungo hit, receive a pitched ball, or receive a pitched ball that bounces at least once before reaching the batting area. Three strikes and three outs apply, with as many innings as time permits.
6. When a player decides to perform a fungo hit, the teacher should stress the need to toss the ball upward, let it bounce once, and then swing.

7. There are no balls or fouls called in the game.
8. Forum - Individuals identify the pros and cons of using different batting techniques.
9. Whenever possible, students hitting home runs should be given the opportunity to carve or write their initials on the bat.
10. Group Discussion Question - Was it helpful to have a choice in the form of pitching, or did it increase the likelihood that one team would only self-hit the ball?

HIT THE STICK

England

OUTCOME

Discover ways of performing effectively

DESCRIPTION OF PLAY

Hit the Stick is an adaptation of the English street game "Flies Up." Using a stickball bat, the batter slams the ball down and hits it after the bounce. Fielders work together to retrieve the ball. The ball is fielded by a player who rolls the ball at the bat, which has been placed in front of the home plate. If the ball hits the stick, the batter is out.

PLAYING SPACE

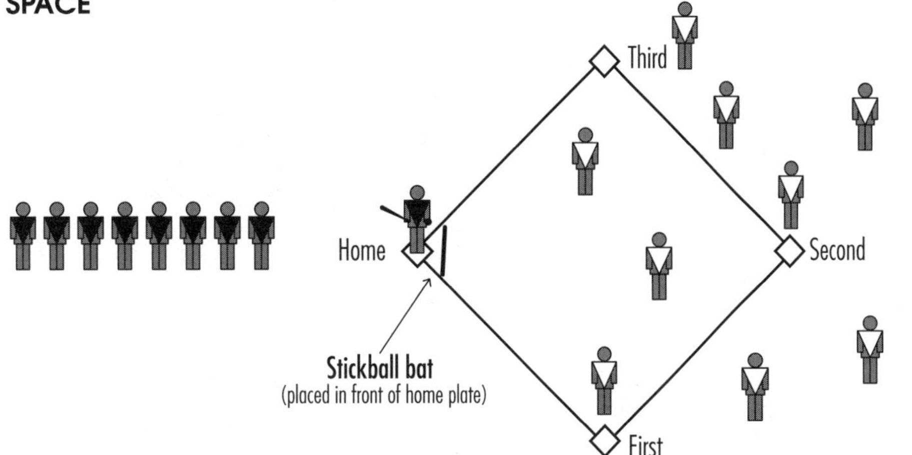

EQUIPMENT

Two stickball bats, pink spaldeens or tennis balls

ESSENTIAL RULES FOR PLAY

1. Divide the students into two groups.
2. A batter, standing at home plate, tosses a tennis ball downward and hits it into an area of fielders after it bounces once.
3. The student who fields the ball stops immediately after the ball is controlled. The runner also stops at the closest base. The fielder then rolls the ball at the stickball bat which has been placed in front of the batting area/base.
4. If the rolled ball hits the bat, the batter is out. A second student from the batting team takes a turn. If the rolled ball does not hit the bat, the batter stays on whichever base was reached before the ball was fielded.
5. If a fly ball is caught, the batter is out.
6. Forum - students assess the degree of force needed to perform a successful bounce when at bat.
7. Teams exchange places when every student from the batting team has completed a turn at bat.
8. Group Discussion Question - Was there one best way to hit the stick from a distance?

QUICK ACTION BASKETBALL

OUTCOME

Seek help from the group

DESCRIPTION OF PLAY

In its early days, basketball was called "Basket Football" or "Football in the Gym." Halftime was called an *inning,* and a goal was called a *touchdown.* In 1891, nine team members were allowed on the court for each team. Today, basketball is played in more than 200 countries worldwide. This basketball shooting activity makes use of a simple rotational system to substitute students quickly and increase participation.

PLAYING SPACE

EQUIPMENT

One basketball and two baskets

ESSENTIAL RULES FOR PLAY

1. The class is divided into four groups. Each group forms a side-by-side line along the wall so that two groups are on each side of the court.
2. The student standing at the end of each line enters the basketball court area. The ball is tossed upward or bounced on the floor randomly by the teacher to begin play.
3. Players attempt to score baskets for their team by dribbling and passing the ball to their line of teammates, who use a return pass in order to score.
4. After each score, all four original players immediately return to the end of their respective group's line, and the next student in each line immediately moves into the court.
5. The students standing in the sidelines move one step to the right to accommodate their returning classmate.
6. There are no jump balls. If two students tie up the ball at the same time, the teacher tosses the ball off the closest backboard.

7. Forum - Students discuss and demonstrate effective basketball passes for long and short distances.
8. Extension - Two students from each line enter the court at the same time.
9. Group Discussion Question - Which shots were more frequently used to increase the likelihood of receiving a quick basket?

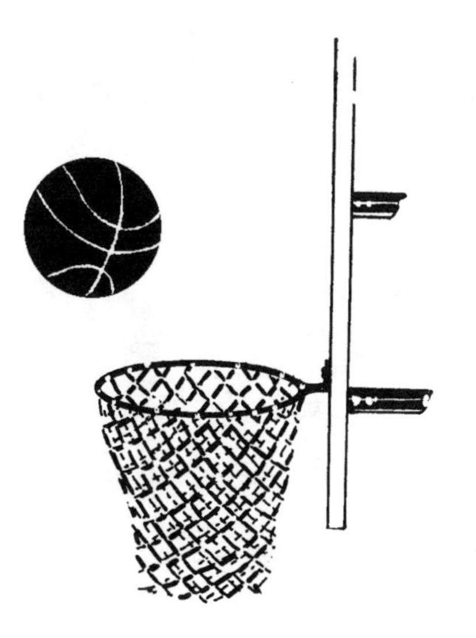

KORFBALL

Holland

OUTCOME

Propose alternative rules for play

DESCRIPTION OF PLAY

Popularized in Holland by Nico Broeukheuysen, a schoolmaster in Amsterdam in 1902, two teams of 12 players each are positioned on three separate playing areas and throw a soccer ball through each area in order to score a basket attached to the top of a post 11-1/2 feet high. There is no backboard. It is one of the only coeducational games played competitively.

PLAYING AREA

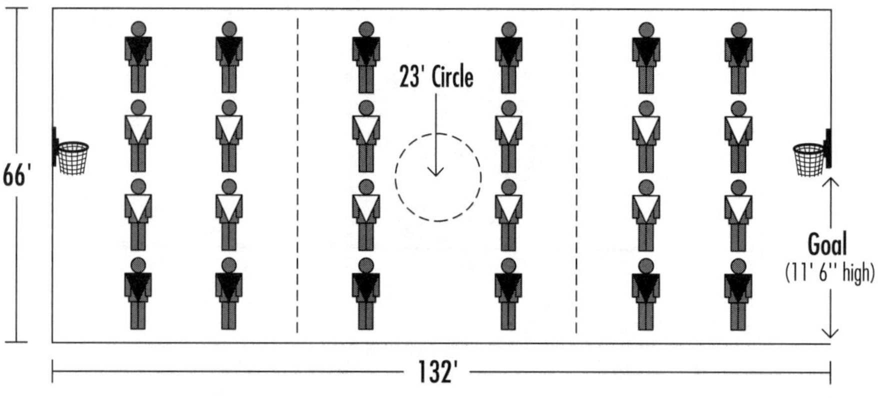

EQUIPMENT

One soccer ball, two basketball hoops raised to 11 feet, 6 inches, cones or tape to divide the three zone areas, and pinnies or jerseys to distinguish teams

ESSENTIAL RULES FOR PLAY

1. Divide the playing area into three separate playing areas. Four players from each team are positioned in each area (two boys and two girls in each zone).
2. Play begins when the teacher throws the ball out of the 23-foot center circle. All players are at least 11-1/2 feet from the thrower.
3. Players advance the ball by throwing it to other teammates. Students may not throw from one division across the center division to the opposite end area. The pass must first go to a center player, and then to the goal area. No player may run with the ball or hand the ball to another teammate. The ball is moved by hand movements only.
4. The defense may not snatch the ball, knock it out of the other team's hands, or interfere, other than to intercept a pass.
5. When a ball is thrown out of bounds, a line throw is awarded to the opposite team at the spot the ball left the playing field. All players must be a minimum of 7 feet

away from the thrower.

6. A penalty throw is awarded to the team not making a foul. Players take a shot from a mark 13 feet in front of the basket. Each goal counts as one point.
7. Play continues for two 15-minute halves.
8. Forum - Players may call for a forum to discuss the addition of several rules (e.g., a 3-second time limit while in possession of the ball, playing with more than one ball, or allowing three steps with the ball before releasing a pass).
9. Group Discussion Question - Did all four players in each zone participate actively during the game, or can a rule be added to increase the likelihood of this in future games?

FOUR SEASON BALL

International

OUTCOME

Develop group strategies

DESCRIPTION OF PLAY

The world's four most popular sports are unique because of the type of ball used and the type of motor skill executed to move the ball forward or to complete a pass. In this activity, two groups of students make use of a variety of balls and try to complete a predetermined number of consecutive passes among teammates before the opposite group can achieve the number.

PLAYING SPACE

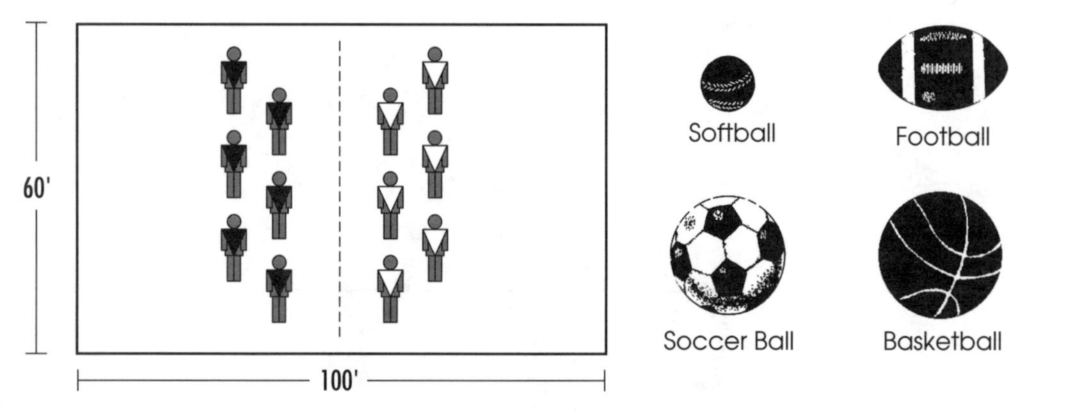

EQUIPMENT

One football, one basketball, one soccer ball, and one softball or baseball, and pinnies or jerseys to distinguish players on two teams

ESSENTIAL RULES FOR PLAY

1. All students are organized in two teams of six to eight players. The game begins with the teacher tossing up either a basketball, softball, football, or a soccer ball between two opposing students in the center of the playing area.
2. Whichever team gains possession of the toss begins to pass the ball in the appropriate manner (i.e., soccer instep kick, basketball chest or bounce pass, football forward pass, or softball overhead throw) to other team players.
3. Each time a player receives a pass, that individual calls out the number.
4. The opposite team tries to intercept the ball and begin their own series of consecutive passes.
5. Both teams must decide upon a "magic number" to reach with a particular ball, before the teacher tosses up the next ball for play. Therefore, the teams may decide to play for five consecutive passes using the soccer ball, and ten passes when throwing a softball.
6. Forum - Students use a clipboard, paper, and marker to draw the positions and running patterns for the greatest likelihood of consecutive passes.
7. Group Discussion Question - Did each team concede gracefully when the opposing group was successful, and which strategy was most effective?

RUN AWAY ROUNDERS

OUTCOME

Celebrate peaceful competition

DESCRIPTION OF PLAY

Run Away Rounders is a modified version of the English game of Rounders. Many sport historians believe that American baseball was a version of Rounders and the popular English sport called *Cricket*. The rules are similar to softball. The student at bat hits a ball into the field and uses base-running skills to run around four posts (or cones) in order to score rounders.

PLAYING SPACE

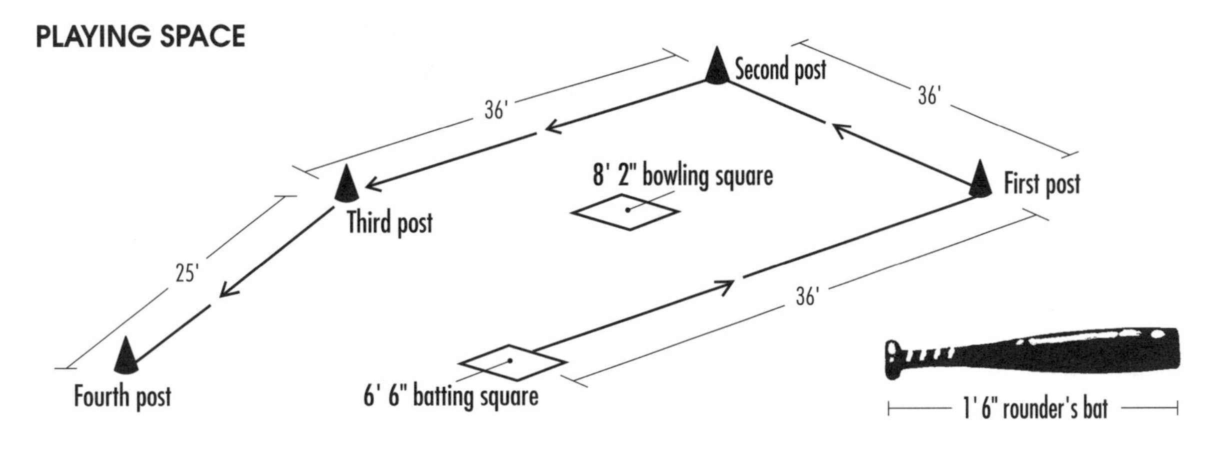

EQUIPMENT

One rounder's bat, or a bat that has been shortened to 18 inches long, a tennis ball, and four cones

ESSENTIAL RULES FOR PLAY

1. Divide students into two teams. One team is positioned in the playing field and the other is at bat.
2. The batsman (i.e., batter) may position him- or herself anywhere within the batting square (i.e., batter's box). This student is permitted to take one step over the sides of the batting square as well as the backline. He or she may not step over the front line. The bat is 1 foot, 6 inches long and is held in one hand.
3. The ball must be pitched between the head and knees and within reach of the bat. When a good pitch is thrown, the batsman must attempt to hit it and run around the four posts. If the batsman misses the third pitch, he or she may still attempt to run around the four posts. Therefore, it is impossible for the batsman to strike out, although the catcher can throw the runner out at first base.
4. Balls not pitched in the designated area are called "no hit" balls. If three "no hit" balls occur, the student scores a "rounder."
5. The pitcher is referred to as the *bowler* and must pitch using the underhand technique

similar to softball.

6. A team at bat is allowed three outs before changing roles with the fielding team.
7. Forum - Students participate in a discussion focusing on fielding strategies.
8. Group Discussion Question - Did individuals feel less stressed knowing that the player could still run to first base even if he or she missed the third strike?

ALMOST ULTIMATE

OUTCOME

Increase group endurance

DESCRIPTION OF PLAY

Ultimate Frisbee™ was first played by a group of high school students in Maplewood, New Jersey. They used the Columbia High School parking lot. This modified version is an active, flying disc game that can be played with a large number of students or with small class populations. The game can also be played inside when a foam flying disc is used. The objective is to make a goal by successfully throwing a disc to a teammate who is standing behind the goal line.

PLAYING SPACE

EQUIPMENT

One flying disc and four cones for goals

ESSENTIAL RULES FOR PLAY

1. *The Grip* - As in any other sport, the proper grip is important. Hold the disc with the thumb on top and index finger just under the rim. The middle finger is extended toward the center with the ring finger and little finger curled back against the rim. The feet should be the same width as the shoulders with the throwing side aimed at the player you want to catch it.

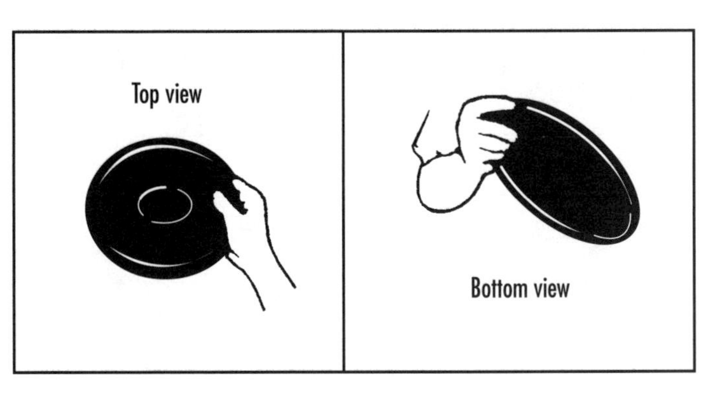

2. *Across the Body Throw* - Begin the throw with the arm extended toward the target and roll the disc into the body as the arm is brought back. The wrist and forearm should be coiled like a spring. Keep the edge away from the body tilted slightly down and the edge toward the target slightly raised.

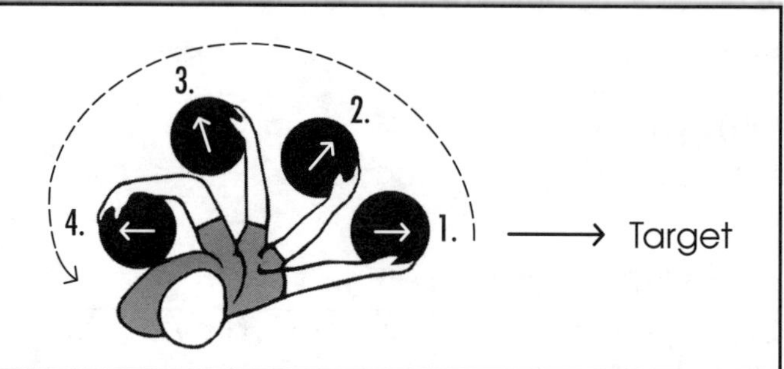

3. Ultimate Frisbee consists of two teams of seven players on a field 40 x 70 yards with 25-yard endzones. In Almost Ultimate, students are divided into two groups of 10 to 12 players. Play begins with the two groups situated on opposite sides of the playing area. One student throws a flying disc (a throw-off) to the receiving team.
4. The receiving team's players must be standing on their goal line until the disc is released. The throwing team may not touch the disc until it has been touched by the receiving team.
5. The receiving team may catch the disc or allow it to fall to the ground without touching it. The receiving team begins passing the disc to teammates. If, however, the receiving team does not secure the disc, the throwing team has possession.
6. Play continues with the students throwing the disc down the field to a teammate who has moved behind his or her goal area. To score a goal, the disc must be passed at least three times on its way to crossing into the goal area.
7. No student may run, step, or hand the disc to a teammate. The disc must be thrown.
8. The opposite team can gain possession of the disc by intercepting and catching a thrown disc, by striking a thrown disc and causing it to fall to the ground, or if the receiving team makes contact but does not catch the disc.
9. Students in possession of the disc may pivot on one foot while throwing the disc.
10. The defending team players may not guard a student closer than 3 feet.
11. Forum - Students outline an offense strategy on paper and implement the strategy on a given team signal.
12. Play continues for four quarters. After each goal is scored, the team gaining the point performs a throw-off to the opposite team.
13. Extension - *Group Freestyle Challenge* - Groups of six players perform as many innovative throws, catches, and moves as possible within a 1-minute period and are judged by other classmates.
14. Group Discussion Question - Who can identify other sports that require continuous movement?

FOUR TARGET FRISBEE

OUTCOME

Share responsibility for constructing equipment

DESCRIPTION OF PLAY

In 1948 Fred Morrison, a carpenter from the USA, created a small plastic flying disc called the *Flying Saucer.* He sold the concept to Wham-O, a San Gabriel, California company who renamed it *Frisbee,™* as it is called today. In this activity, four groups of students create a unique goal marker to defend and use a variety of passes to score against each other's target.

PLAYING SPACE

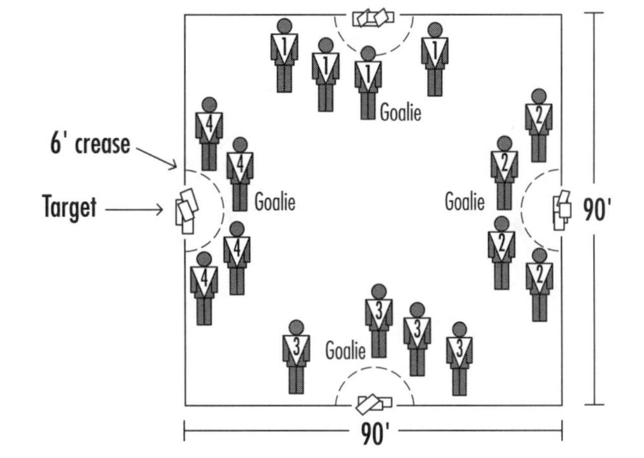

EQUIPMENT

Construction paper, markers, masking tape, and one flying disc

ESSENTIAL RULES FOR PLAY

1. Organize the students in four teams of 1s, 2s, 3s, and 4s. Distribute five sheets of construction paper, markers, and masking tape to each team and challenge the groups to design a target. If possible, use bright neon paper for added incentive. All sheets of paper must connect or overlap in some way. Each target must be placed 3 feet from the ground and can be positioned anywhere along the sideline of the team's defending area.
2. Three players from each team enter the playing area and one member from each team assumes the role of goalie. Play begins with each team selecting a number between one and twenty. The team guessing the number closest to the teacher's predetermined number is awarded the disc and may begin passing.
3. The disc is thrown from student to student. No player may run with the disc or hand the disc to a teammate. Each player in possession of the disc has only 3 seconds to pass to a teammate.
4. The defensive teams try to intercept passes and score against any of the other team's targets. No defensive player may guard an opponent closer than 3 feet or snatch the disc, or enter an opponent's 6-foot crease in front of the goal.

5. Whenever a team scores, the next consecutive team's goalie is given possession of the disc. For example, if the 4s score a goal (1 point), then the goalie from the 1s is given the disc and play immediately resumes.
6. Play continues for four 10-minute segments with substitutions at the end of each segment.
7. Forum - Students reflect on the difficulty of hitting their target based on its design.
8. Extension - Depending on the availability of space, three flying discs can be added to the game.
9. Group Discussion Question - Were there particular targets that conveyed special artistic abilities that reflected their team's characteristics?

TEAM DECK TENNIS

OUTCOME

Accept new challenges

DESCRIPTION OF PLAY

Deck Tennis was created by Cleve F. Schaffer to be played on ship decks. It is an English throwing game involving a deck tennis ring, a 4-foot, 8-inch-high net, and a neutral zone. Although commonly played by two players on a 40-foot-long court, team deck tennis can involve large class populations when the net is raised to 5 feet, 8 inches and the size of the court area is extended.

PLAYING SPACE

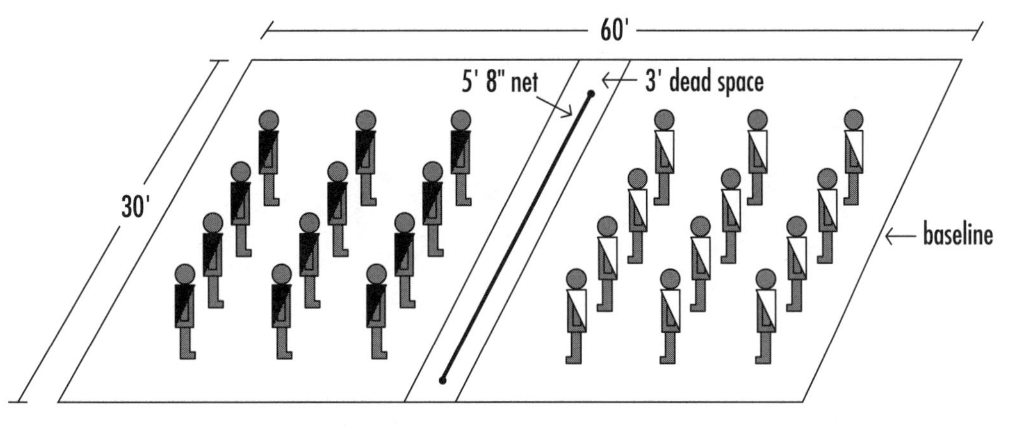

EQUIPMENT

Volleyball net, standards, and a deck tennis ring

ESSENTIAL RULES FOR PLAY

1. Divide the students into two teams. Teams organize their players in line formations. Play begins when a student stands behind the baseline and uses a sidearm serve to propel the ring into the opposing team's court. Individuals take turns serving. A serve that hits the net and lands in the neutral or "dead space" area should be replayed.
2. The opposite team members attempt to catch the ring by using only one hand, and the return toss must be made with the hand that caught the ring. Play continues until the ring is not caught or it lands in the opponent's dead space.
3. No overhead smashes are allowed. Students must use a sidearm throw with an overhand grip.
4. Scoring is performed as in volleyball (i.e., points can only be made from the serving side, and the team must win by two points). Teams agree to play to 16 or 21 points.
5. Forum - Students reposition group members for effective play.

6. The following result in the loss of a serve or winning a point:
    - The ring touches a student's wrist or body part other than the hand
    - Throwing the ring out of bounds or beyond the serving line
    - Failing to catch the ring
    - Catching the ring with more than one hand
    - Stepping on or over the baseline when serving
    - Taking more than one step after catching the ring
    - Using a throw other than a sidearm throw to return the ring
7. Group Discussion Question - Did each team see an increased level of play after the Forum and have the opportunity to perform the sidearm throw during game play?

CULTURALLY DIVERSE REALLY WILD RELAYS

International

OUTCOME

Identify group strengths and talents

DESCRIPTION OF PLAY

Relay races increased the endurance levels of the ancient Greek message runners. Unlike most relays that require every student in a line formation to participate, Really Wild Relays encourages the teams to choose two or three individuals from their group to perform the task. All relay tasks are aimed at promoting teamwork while emphasizing strength, balance, power, or cooperative movement.

PLAYING SPACE

English Wheelbarrow

EQUIPMENT

Tennis balls, beach balls, or playground balls

ESSENTIAL RULES FOR PLAY

Forum - Each group decides which students will enter the event based on the key element inherent in that particular race. This factor is announced by the teacher (e.g., "The first relay focuses on strength, so choose your players based on their ability to exert force for an extended period of time"). Each group is responsible for one entry per race.

RELAYS EMPHASIZING STRENGTH

1. *English Wheelbarrow* - Two students grasp the legs of a third student who is in a push-up position. The three students work together (after changing positions) to move around a designated cone and return to their group.
2. *Greek Rescue Carry* - Two students stand facing each other and firmly grasp each other's wrists. A third student uses the other two students' arms as a seat, sitting on the two arms. The third student's arms are positioned around the shoulders of the other two students. The third student is carried around the designated cone and returned to the group.
3. *Roman Crab Race* – Two students sit one behind the other facing the designated cone. The front player leans back and grasps the second player's ankles, while the second partner is leaning back and is placing his or her hands on the floor behind the body. On signal, both students raise their buttocks off the floor and race to the turning line, then back to the starting line. Repeat using three students.

RELAYS EMPHASIZING COOPERATIVE MOVEMENT

4. *Greek Chariot Race* - Two students standing side-by-side grasp wrists to form a front line. A third student stands behind the other two students and grasps each front student's outside hand to simulate a chariot with two horses and one rider. The group of three runs around the designated cone and returns to their group.
5. *Australian This Sway and That* - Two students grasp each other's waists and move forward by swaying both partners' right legs to the right, followed by both left legs to the left, and so on, to the designated cone and then return to the group.
6. *New Zealand Beach Ball Carry* - Two students stand back-to-back with a beach ball or similar ball placed between their backs. Together, the two students move down and around the cone attempting not to drop the ball. Both students must replace the ball if a drop occurs, before moving to the designated cone and back to their group.
7. *Japanese Three Legged Race* - The left ankles of three students are tied together. The students must move together to a designated cone and return to their group.
8. *Irish Pilot Race* - Three students lock elbows so that the two end students are running backward while the middle player faces front and pilots the trio's running path to the designated cone and back.

RELAYS EMPHASIZING BALANCE

9. *English Hop to It* - Two students extend their inside arms around each other's shoulders so that the inside legs are side-by-side. Each student then grasps his or her own outside ankle using their outside arm, in order that both students are balancing on the inside leg. The two students hop together to and around the designated cone and return to their group.
10. *Italian Triple Hop* - Three students form a behind line. The front student raises his or her left leg behind, and the second student grasps it using the left hand. The second student repeats the action to the third. The third student raises the left leg. On signal, they hop to the designated turning line, then return to the start.

RELAYS EMPHASIZING POWER

11. *Belgian Partner Long Jump* - Two students stand side-by-side at the start of the race. One student performs a standing long jump using the common 2-foot take-off. The partner quickly moves up to his or her side and performs a second standing long jump. The two partners continue until they have jumped around the designated cone and then return to their team. Extension - Ladder Jump is played in England using four students.
12. *Australian Kangaroo Jump* - Two students stand side-by-side at the start of the race and clasp inside hands or wrists. A piece of cardboard is placed between each person's feet. On signal, they jump forward to the designated cone while maintaining hand grips and keeping the paper between their feet.
13. *Greek Engine Pulling The Train* - Four players hold on to the waists of their group members. All groups form a line at the starting line. On the teacher's signal, all groups perform 2-foot jumps to a designated turning line. To increase the pace, the first player in each line becomes the "engine" by coordinating the speed of the jumps.
14. Group Discussion Question - How important was the distribution of strengths and talents for a group's success?

TEAM ROCK, PAPER, SCISSORS

Japan

OUTCOME

Actively play for luck and chance

DESCRIPTION OF PLAY

Originating in Japan, this classic game has the distinction of being played by either individuals or teams throughout the world. The following team approach requires all students to react quickly and take chase, or become a member of the opposite team.

PLAYING SPACE

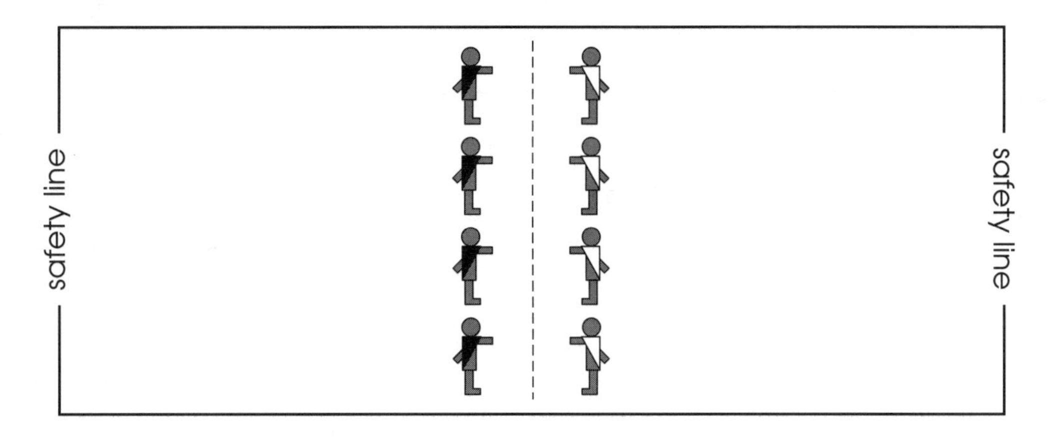

EQUIPMENT

Large poster and markers

ESSENTIAL RULES FOR PLAY

1. Construct a large poster with the words, "rock breaks scissor, scissor cuts paper, paper covers rock" in close proximity to the playing area for all students to see.
2. Divide the players into two teams and explain that the object of the game is to have the greatest number of players on one team.
3. Discuss the symbols used for play by demonstrating a clenched fist (the rock), extending the index and middle fingers (the scissors), and the paper (an open flat hand). Remind students that the rock beats scissors because it breaks them, the scissors beat paper because it cuts it, and the paper beats rock because it covers it.
4. Forum - Both teams separate, form a huddle, and decide upon one symbol. All players then advance to the middle of the playing area, and "toe the line" so that both teams are facing each other. One hand of each player is behind the back.
5. The teacher calls "Rock, Paper, Scissors." On the word "scissors," both teams display their symbol in front of the body. The team with the winning symbol immediately chases members from the opposite team, who quickly turn and retreat back to

their team's safety line. All players tagged before reaching the safety line become members of the opposite team.

6. In the event that both teams display the same symbol, both teams quickly reassemble and decide to show a different symbol or to repeat their first symbol.
7. Extension - In Japan, the game *JAN-KEM-PO* (stone-paper-scissors) is sometimes played in a team relay formation. Runners from two teams are positioned in opposite corners of the playing field. On the teacher's signal, the first player from each team begins to run around the square. Whenever and wherever two runners meet, they stop and say *JAN-KEM-PO.* On the word *PO* they display either a stone, paper, or scissors symbol. The winning player continues to run and a new player from the losing player's team quickly enters the game. A losing player from either team is eliminated and stands in a designated area in front or to the side of the endline. Play continues until all players have had the opportunity to run and all players meet an opposing player. The object is to be the team with the least number of eliminated players. Players sometimes meet in the center, but may also meet in close proximity to the other team's beginning mark.

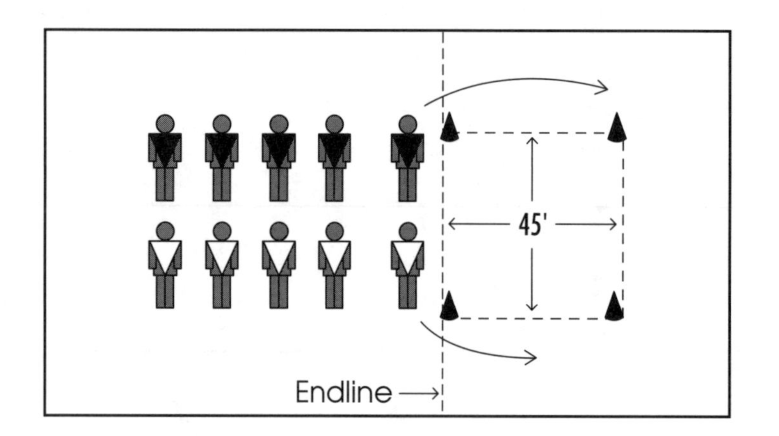

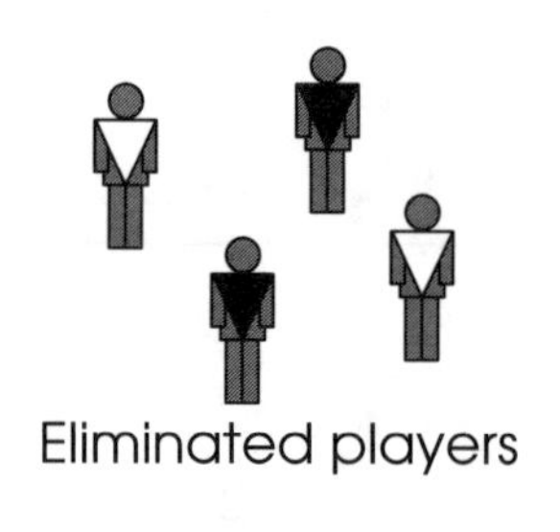

8. Extension - In Korea, the game *KAWI-PAWI-PO* is played the same way with the following exception; *KAWI* means scissors, *PAWI* means stone, and *PO* means cloth. Scissors can cut cloth (scissors win), cloth can wrap up stone (cloth wins), and stones can break scissors (stone wins).
9. Group Discussion Question - What additional sports do we participate in today that are based largely on luck and chance?

Netherlands

OUTCOME

Adjust to different situations

DESCRIPTION OF PLAY

Rip flag activities, very popular in the Netherlands, can be played in limited spaces or outdoors with ample moving space. When flag football belts are not available, discarded beach balls may be cut into their colored sections and situated so that they hang 5 to 7 inches from the student's pants or back pocket. All activities reinforce the strategies used to move away from an opponent (e.g., darting, dodging, dashing, feinting, or side-stepping).

PLAYING SPACE

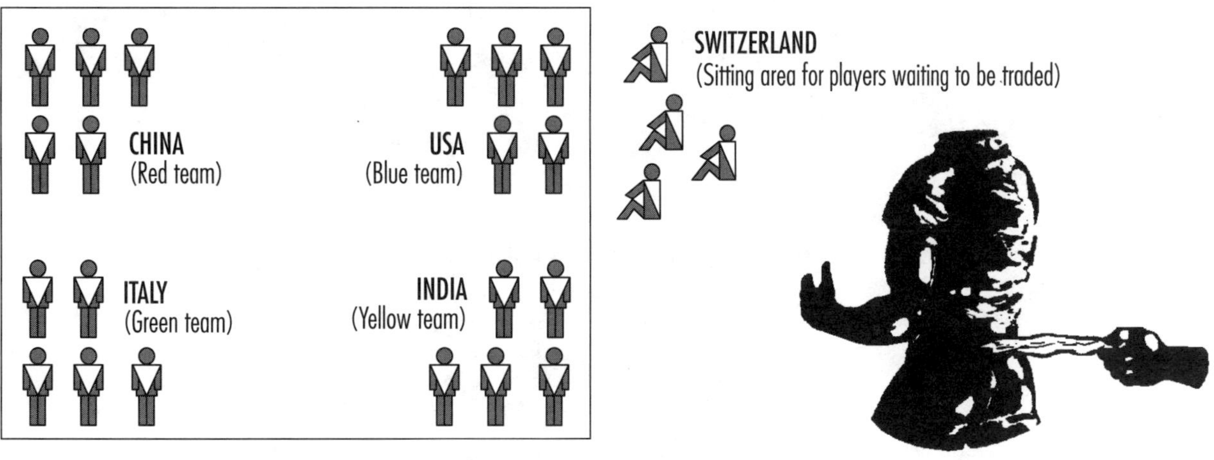

EQUIPMENT

Rip flags of four different colors or stripes of color from beach balls

ESSENTIAL RULES FOR PLAY

1. Students are divided into four groups. Each group is given a particular color and is situated in a different corner of the playing space. An area is also designated for students to sit after their flag is pulled.
2. On the teacher's signal, all four colors attempt to grab and remove a flag from the other team's players. After a 1- or 2-minute time period, depending on the size of the playing area, the teacher signals for the action to stop.
3. Individuals having their flag pulled should be sitting in the pre-named area (e.g., Switzerland). The student having pulled the greatest number of flags selects students from the designated sitting area to join his or her team, and those students assume the same color flag as the student performing the selection.
4. The student acquiring the next highest number of flags selects students, and so on until all students have been selected. All groups return to their corners.

5. The teacher gives the signal for action. The process is repeated until one group has acquired all of the students and, subsequently, one color remains on the playing field. For example, if a student from the Blue team pulls five flags, then five students from the designated sitting area join the Blue team.
6. After the students have acquired a basic understanding of the game, have each group designate themselves as a country. For example, the Green team represents Italy, the Blue team represents the USA, and so on.
7. Forum - Groups practice dodging opponents in order to evade a pulled flag.
8. Group Discussion Question - Identify several sports that require players to evade an opponent.

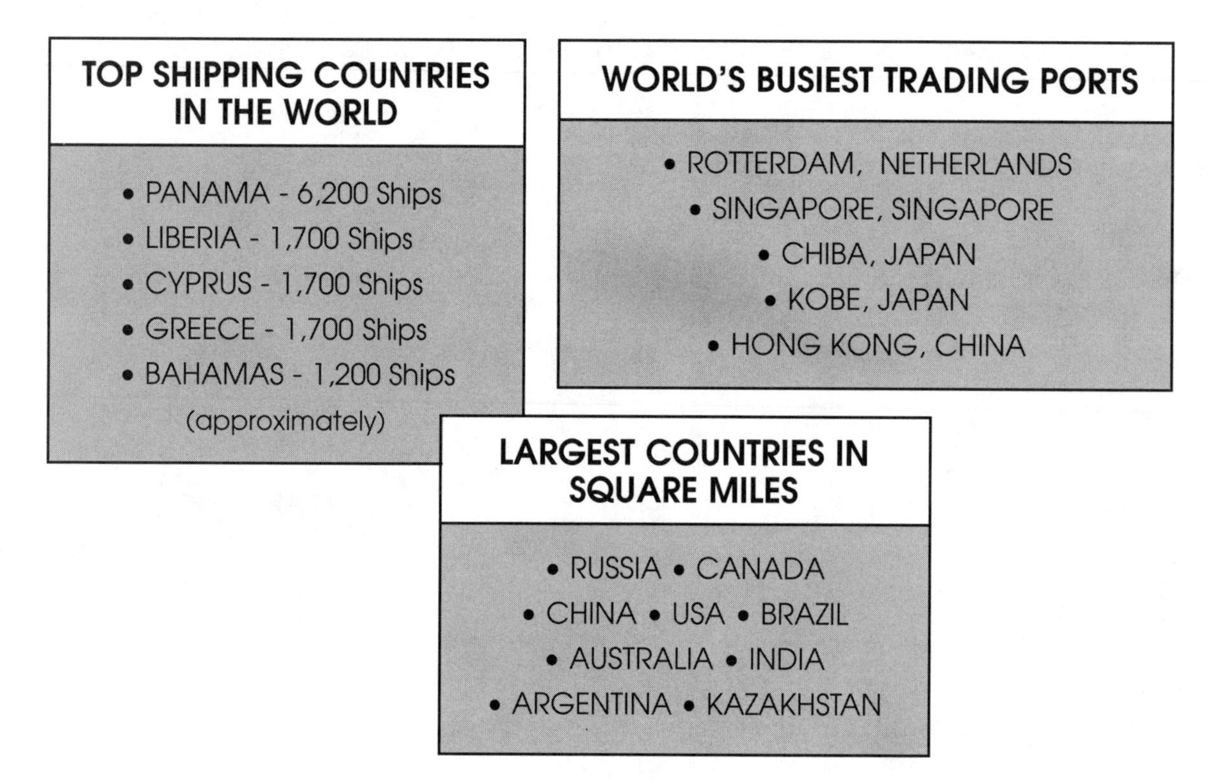

TOSS AND CATCH NETS

Philippines

OUTCOME

Behave autonomously

DESCRIPTION OF PLAY

Nets have been used in numerous games and sports. The most common use is to catch a puck or ball that has been kicked through a goal. Many teachers of the 1920s were trained at tying rope to create a net for game play. In the Philippines, this activity involves groups of four to six students manipulating 12-foot nylon nets and a beach ball is tossed from net to net in a competitive or cooperative activity.

PLAYING SPACE

EQUIPMENT

Nylon nets or discarded bed sheets, beachball or ball of similar weight

ESSENTIAL RULES FOR PLAY

1. Divide the students into groups of four to six students.
2. Each group is given a 12-foot nylon rope net. This net can be purchased at hardware stores or boating supplies stores at a minimal cost.
3. One group is given a beach ball or a ball of similar weight.
4. On the teacher's signal, groups cooperate to pass the ball from net to net.
5. Extension - The class cooperates to pass the ball back and forth as quickly as possible within a specific time limit.
6. Extension - The class cooperates to pass the ball a designated number of times in succession without dropping the ball.
7. Forum - Students compose a list of rules for cooperative or competitive game for whole group participation.
8. Group Discussion Question - How important was it to move in a whole group effort in order to catch the ball?

HORSE RACE

England

OUTCOME

Describe group conduct

DESCRIPTION OF PLAY

The sport of horseback riding, originating in England, dates back to when men first domesticated horses. Thoroughbred horse racing in England is often called "the sport of kings." The earliest recorded equestrian event was show-jumping. It took place in Dublin, Ireland, in 1864. Horse racing is one of America's oldest sports. The game of Horse Race is based on chance. Students work cooperatively to construct the materials needed to play the game and are responsible for organizing all aspects of the activity. The objective is to be the first "horse" to complete the grid race track.

PLAYING SPACE

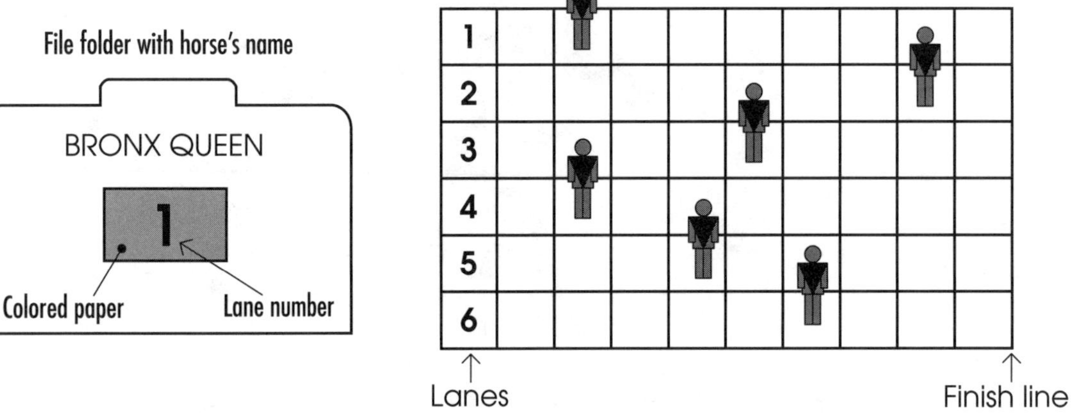

EQUIPMENT

Chalk or tape, construction paper, a die or a spinner

ESSENTIAL RULES FOR PLAY

1. The class is divided into four groups. One group is responsible for lining the floor with chalk or tape to represent a large grid. Group Two decorates a table with construction paper signs to identify the different horses' names. Group Three sits behind the table and collects "bets." Group Four uses dice or a spinner and calls the numbers to advance the horses.
2. All students may place a "bet" before each race. This is possible by approaching the table and selecting one construction paper square that is coded according to the lane and horse.
3. All four groups take turns representing the horses. The die is rolled and the student standing in that numbered grid advances one space.
4. The first horse (or number) to reach the table is the winner of the race. All students

holding that number return to the betting booth table where they receive a novelty item (e.g., sugarless gum or candy).

5. Possible student-selected names to represent horses - Whirl Away, Native Dancer, Evan's Choice, No Disrespect, Troublemaker, Puerto Rican Pride, San Juan Strongman, Asian Wonder, Black Beauty, Equal Time, African Queen, Caroline's Child.
6. Forum - Students discuss the importance of luck verses strategy.
7. Group Discussion Question - Did all members play an important role in this activity?

JAPANESE GROUP COMBATIVE CHALLENGES

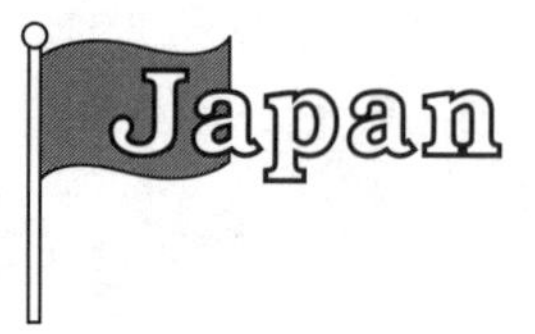

OUTCOME

Contribute to group efforts

DESCRIPTION OF PLAY

Literally, *judo* means "gentle way." Judo emerged in Japan from *ju-jitsu,* a method of unarmed combat. Judo is a formal sport with partners *(aite)* bowing to each other before and after each match. Group Combative Challenges allows individuals from two groups to perform combative tasks and receive points for their respective teams. Challengers enter a circular contest area and participate in bouts (i.e., a contest of a set length) emphasizing either pushing, pulling, reaction time, or strength-related skills. The word *challenges* originated in 14th century English, meaning "inviting to a contest."

PLAYING SPACE

16' – 20'

EQUIPMENT

Wooden or plastic pins, one playground ball, rip flags

ESSENTIAL RULES FOR PLAY

1. Divide the students into two groups. One student from each group enters a 16- to 20-foot ring. Combative challengers enter the bout ring and either shake hands or *rei* (bow).
2. *Japanese Pushing Bout: Pin Push* (Wooden or plastic pins are placed around a 16- to 20-foot diameter to make a bout ring). Students from each team enter and shake hands. The two students place their hands on each other's shoulders. On the teacher's *(sensei)* signal *(hajime),* the challengers attempt to push each other in such a way as to knock down a pin. Play continues until all students from both teams have participated.
3. *Pulling Bout: Ball Tug of War* - Students from each team enter the ring and shake hands. The teacher places (holds) the ball between the two students. One student grasps the ball around the top and the bottom, while the other grasps the ball around its sides. Both students have their fingers clasped, and the ball should be hugged tightly. The teacher steps back and signals for the bout to begin. Both students attempt to gain possession of the ball.

4. *Reaction Time Bout: Grab a Flag* - Students from each team enter the bout ring (a gymnastic mat) and shake hands. Both students are wearing a flag (a cloth strip) in their back pocket, extending from their pants/shorts. On the teacher's signal, the two students attempt to grab the flag from a standing position, or while starting on their hands and knees, before the end of a 15-second period.
5. *Strength Bout* - Students assume a kneeling position on one gymnastic mat *(tatami).* On the teacher's signal, both try to move the other challenger off the mat before the end of a 10-second time period. *Kuzushi* means to force an opponent to lose his or her balance.
6. Scoring - Successful challengers receive three points for their team. This is called a *Koka.* A draw should be declared in bouts in which the two students appear equally matched.
7. Forum - Teams take turns sending one combative challenger into the ring. Depending on who is selected by the first team, the second team's choice is decided after some discussion among group members.
8. Group Discussion Question - What factors helped each group to select the player that would enter the ring?

JAPANESE TERMINOLOGY

aite = opponent
ashi = leg/foot
ashi-yube = toes
atama = head
fusegi = defense
hajime = instruction to begin
hara = stomach
hiza = knee
jikan = time out period
ju = gentle
kake = maximum power
kao = face
keikoku = warning from official
koka = a score
kubi = neck
mata = inside of thigh
morote = two hands
nage = a pushing action
randori = practice
rei = the bow
sensei = teacher
tatami = mat
tekubi = wrist
ude = arm

JAPANESE COUNTING

English	Japanese	Sound
one	ichi	*itchy*
two	ni	*knee*
three	san	*sun*
four	shi	*she*
five	go	*go*
six	rocko	*rock*
seven	shichi	*shi-chi*
eight	hachi	*hat-chi*
nine	kyu	*coo*
ten	ju	*ju*

COMBATIVE SPORTS PLAYED TODAY

- **AIKIDO** - *Uses flowing techniques to throw opponent off balance*
- **BOXING** • **FENCING**
- **JUJITSU** - *Includes throws, kicks, and punches*
- **JUDO** • **KARATE** • **WRESTLING**
- **KENDO** - *Japanese sword art*

AWESOME ARCHWAY

OUTCOME

Foster a sense of interdependence

DESCRIPTION OF PLAY

Groups of eight or more students on a team work cooperatively to maneuver through an arch, which is formed by two members of the group, before a second team can complete a movement. The word *arch* stems from the French word *arche* meaning curve or bow.

PLAYING SPACE

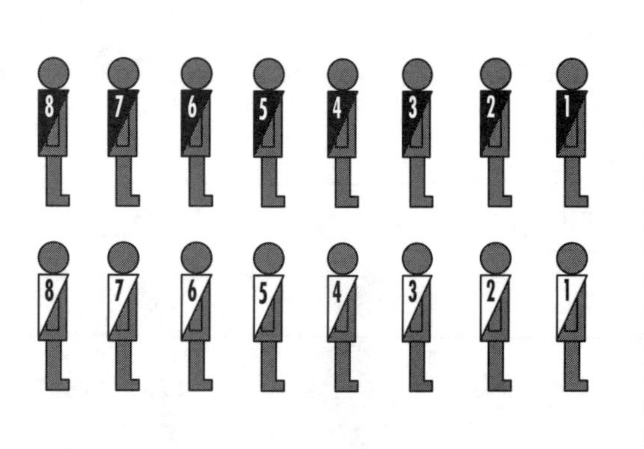

EQUIPMENT

Dynamic music for extension activity

ESSENTIAL RULES FOR PLAY

1. Divide the students into two or more groups of eight or more players. Each group forms a single-file line by spacing its members approximately one body length from each other. Individuals are numbered consecutively.
2. The teacher calls two numbers. These two students from each line run to a designated area in front of the lines and form an arch by joining hands overhead. The remainder of the group runs in numerical order through the arch and returns to their starting position. The students forming the arch must also return to their original positions in line.
3. The team with all players in their original position first scores one point. Students agree to play to five or ten points.
4. Extension - Use a circle formation instead of a line to perform a popular English version.
5. Extension - French Arch is a well-known French dance in which small groups of students scatter throughout the activity area. Two members of each group form an arch. All other members move and dance to dynamic music. Whenever a group member moves through the arch, he or she must change their type of movement.
6. Group Discussion Question - What factors slowed the group?

ALL WET SPORT ACQUATICO

Italy

OUTCOME

Accommodate group needs

DESCRIPTION OF PLAY

Swimming is one of the most popular sports around the world. Plato, the famous Greek philosopher, wrote that a man's education was not finished until he could read, write, and swim. In this Italian activity, groups select individuals from their team to perform novelty swimming tasks. All levels of swimming ability should be able to participate.

PLAYING SPACE

Ball Clutch Event

EQUIPMENT

Playground balls and plastic cups

ESSENTIAL RULES FOR PLAY

1. The students are divided into groups of six or more students. The events are posted or announced to the class.
2. Forum - Each group decides which student(s) will participate in an event based on the key element of that particular event. The teacher determines the distance of each event depending on the class' swimming abilities.
3. Groups are responsible for judging the events.
4. *Backward Swim Event* - While lying on the stomach in a prone position, participants move in the direction of the feet by applying a reverse arm stroke motion.
5. *Torpedo Race Event* - The student moves forward by making one stoke in a prone position, directly followed by one stroke on his or her back. This motion creates a spinning action as the participant moves forward. The flutter kick is suggested, although any kick may be used.
6. *Ball Clutch Event* - Participants swim forward while holding a playground ball in front of the body.

7. *Leg Grip* - Participants swim forward while holding a ball between their knees.
8. *Douse the Fire Event* - Students swim forward while carrying a plastic cup filled with water. There must be water in the cup at the completion of the race.
9. *Frog Jump Relay* - Two students enter the water. One student is treading water or standing in front of the second student. On the teacher's signal, the student in the rear places his or her hands on the partner's shoulders, which naturally pushes the lead student downward. This student swims over the first partner's body. The student under the water immediately surfaces to perform the same movement. The two students progress down the pool, repeating the task.
10. *Waterbug Relay Event* - Two students enter the water. One student assumes a free-style stroke with the second student holding on to their partner's shoulder. The student in the top position is usually the smaller of the two students. Both students must stay attached while finding the best way to swim down the pool lane.
11. *One Arm Partner Swim* - Two students enter the water and grasp each other's inside elbow. The two students swim together using their outside arms to progress forward.
12. Extension - Partners place their inside arms around each other's shoulders and swim forward.
13. Group Discussion Question - Were individuals well suited for a specific event, or should a change be made when we repeat the activity?

RESCUE ME AQUATIC RELAYS

OUTCOME

Provide or respect leadership

DESCRIPTION OF PLAY

The earliest swimming competition was held in Japan in 36 B.C. In the 1800s, the Japanese Emperor ordered all people to swim and then organized swimming events. Rescue Me Aquatic Relays are used after the student has been introduced to basic lifesaving land assists. The objective is for one student to remove all of his or her group members from the pool as quickly as possible.

PLAYING SPACE

EQUIPMENT

Ring buoy(s) and throwing lines

ESSENTIAL RULES FOR PLAY

1. Students are divided into two to four groups depending on the number of available ring buoys. One student from each group is assigned the role of "rescuer" and stands ready at the side of the pool. All group members enter the pool and tread water approximately 10 to 15 feet from the pool's edge.
2. On the teacher's signal, each rescuer throws a ring buoy and line to one of his or her group members. Only one student should respond to the toss. The group member is carefully pulled to safety.
3. The rescuer continues to throw until all group members are brought to the edge of the pool. The rescuer should ask group members for assistance after towing three group members.
4. Extension - The rescuer uses a kickboard or a towel to perform reaching assists.
5. Group Discussion Question - Who should be the next rescuer?

KICKBOARD WATER POLO

England

OUTCOME

Value perseverance

DESCRIPTION OF PLAY

Water polo was first called aquatic handball, aquatic football, or water soccer during the late 1860s in England. It was originally played in rivers and lakes. In 1870, the sport moved indoors and was brought to America in 1880, where seven players made up a team. The objective of Kickboard Water Polo is to secure goals by throwing a ball and knocking over the opposing team's two kickboard standards. Lane lines can remain intact.

PLAYING SPACE

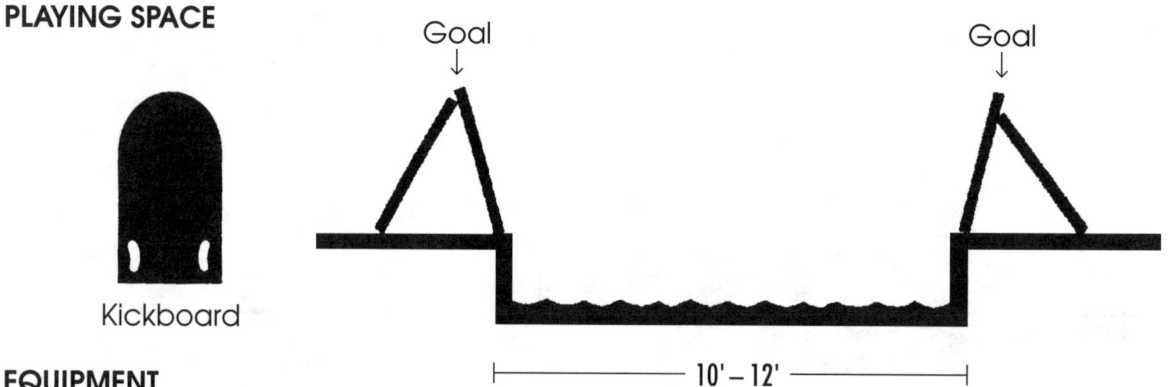

EQUIPMENT

Eight kickboards and one ball

ESSENTIAL RULES FOR PLAY

1. The class is divided into two teams. Depending on the size of the pool, eight to ten students per team is recommended.
2. The goals consist of four kickboards. Each goal has two kickboards that stand up by leaning against each other. A distance of 10 to 12 feet separates the two goals.
3. The goalie is allowed to stand outside of the water to protect the goals. Play is started by having the teacher turn away from the pool momentarily and toss the ball over his or her right shoulder back into the pool.
4. The team that throws a ball and knocks over one side of the kickboard goal is awarded one point. The two kickboards are not reset until both goals are knocked over.
5. The ball may be propelled one-handed, pushed or dribbled through the water, or seized and held with one hand.
6. When two opposing players have secured or tackled the ball at the same time, a whistle is blown and the teacher shouts, "Tied up." The ball is given to the teacher, who repeats the action used to begin play.
7. If lane lines are used, no more than one defensive player is allowed in the area nearest to the goal. No offensive players are allowed in this area.
8. Group Discussion Question - Did you have any problems remaining physically active while playing, and can you identify any aquatic activities to help you get in shape for a 40-minute game?

AMERICAN INDIAN DODGE AND THROW

OUTCOME

Show concern for the welfare of others

DESCRIPTION OF PLAY

The American Indians whittled blocks of wood to serve as targets to practice hunting and aiming skills. In this activity, students use a variety of different throwing techniques to eliminate the opposite team's Indian clubs or players while striving to maintain their own participation in the game.

PLAYING SPACE

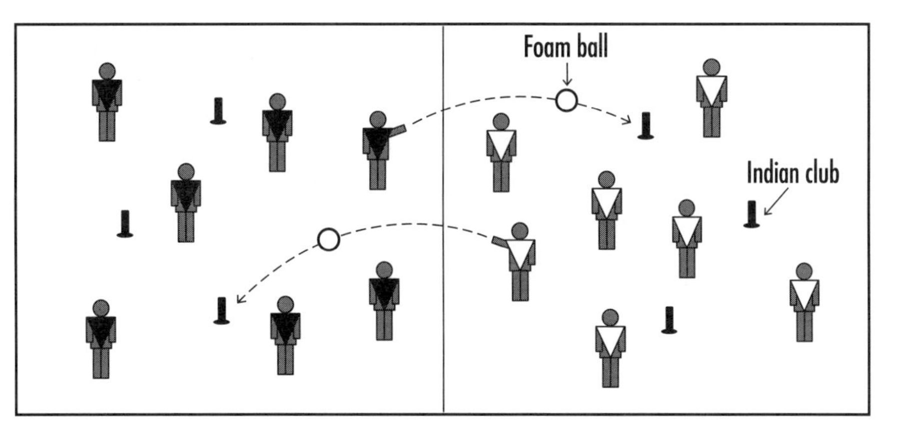

EQUIPMENT

Six Indian clubs and two foam balls

ESSENTIAL RULES FOR PLAY

1. Students are organized in two teams. Each team is given three Indian clubs to place anywhere on their side of the activity area.
2. Both teams are given a foam playground ball and begin action on the teacher's signal.
3. The object is to throw the ball and knock down the other team's Indian clubs or to hit the opposite team's players below the waist. No player may cross the dividing line that separates the two courts.
4. Students dodge the oncoming ball or may catch a thrown ball to avoid being eliminated.
5. The first team to either knock over all three pins or to eliminate all of the opposite team's players is victorious.
6. Forum - Students are given 2 to 3 minutes to determine the best strategy for success based on either the number of remaining players or Indian clubs.
7. The game consists of three complete rounds. All students reenter the game at the

beginning of each round and reflect upon the results of the earlier round to discover the best elimination strategy, placement of the Indian clubs, and the most successful aiming and throwing techniques.

8. Extension - Add a 6-foot square box in each of the playing areas and four corners. When a student is eliminated, he or she is positioned in either of the two boxes on the opponent's side of the court. All players must remain in the box, but may grasp any ball that rolls or is thrown into the box, and may throw it at the pins or the opposite team's players. Hence, eliminated players are still active throughout each round.
9. Group Discussion Question - Were there any strategies used to protect team players from being hit?

ALL SPORT NOVELTY MEETS

OUTCOME

Perform one's own special talents

DESCRIPTION OF PLAY

Novelty Sport Meets give individuals the opportunity to demonstrate their strengths in one particular event while contributing to their team's effort.

PLAYING SPACE

EQUIPMENT

Soccer, basketball, tennis, softball, track, volleyball, and field hockey equipment

ESSENTIAL RULES FOR PLAY

1. The students are divided into groups of four or more. The teacher posts the events for each sport area, depending on the available equipment and space.
2. Forum - Each group of students is responsible for assigning one of its group members to each event.
3. Option One For Organization - Groups volunteer to secure the equipment for one sport area. Group One, for example, organizes and conducts all softball events for the remaining groups. Group Two organizes the activities for the football events, and so on.
4. Option Two For Organization - The class completes one or two events from each sport area during one class period. A decision can also be made to complete all of the basketball events, for example, during one class session.
5. Suggested events include the following:

   a. SOCCER
   - Punt for Distance
   - Place Kick for Accuracy
   - Goal Kick for Accuracy
   - Throw in for Distance

b. FOOTBALL
- Punt for Distance
- Drop Kick for Distance
- Forward Pass for Accuracy
- Forward Pass for Distance

c. BASKETBALL
- Foul Shooting
- Three Point Shots
- Dribble for Time
- Lay up Shots for Time

d. TENNIS
- Serve for Accuracy
- Forehand Volley Against a Wall for Time
- Backhand Volley Against a Wall for Time
- Volley With a Partner for Time

e. SOFTBALL
- Fungo Hit for Distance
- Base Running for Time
- Bat and Run to 1st Base for Time
- Catcher's Throw to 2nd Base for Accuracy

f. TRACK
- 100-yard Dash
- 220-yard Dash
- 120-yard Hurdles
- 220-yard Hurdles

g. VOLLEYBALL
- Serve for Accuracy
- Set With a Partner for Time
- Forearm Pass With a Partner for Time
- Spiking a Ball From a Set for Accuracy

h. FIELD HOCKEY
- Dribble for Distance
- Drive for Accuracy
- Drive for Distance
- Drive at a Goal

PART III
CURRICULUM EXPANSION

CHAPTER

5

Assessing Multicultural Outcomes

ASSESSING INDIVIDUAL AND GROUP INTERACTION WITHIN A MULTICULTURAL SETTING

Typically, educational outcomes address the question, "What should students know and be able to do?" Physical education outcomes also address this query and place importance on the question, "What should the student value?" (NASPE 1995). The word *value* stems from Old French *value* or *valoir* meaning "to be or have worth," and an individual's worth is at the core of this text's multicultural approach. Furthermore, the extent to which any student experiences success within a multicultural or nonmulticultural physical education setting weighs heavily on the student's ability to work independently and in cooperation with peers in order to have worth. When assessing individual and group interaction, and the extent to which an outcome is achieved, the teacher may find it useful to use a rubric that identifies a range of criteria that the student should meet. This text contains three sample rubrics to assist the teacher's efforts.

The purpose of Sample Rubric A is to appraise the extent of positive socialization that one student experiences while interacting with one peer or partner. It is specially designed to be used with activities found in chapter 3. The extent of interaction ranges from a low of one point indicating that the teacher needed to prompt or ask the student to interact with a classmate, to four points, representing excellent interaction. The findings show that some individuals will achieve a perfect score of 40 points, while others need intervention. In Sample Rubric B, the teacher again observes one student's performance throughout a lesson and uses the descriptors to determine the student's success in socializing, mingling, and fraternizing with a small or large group of peers. Like Rubric A, the student can achieve 40 points by always exhibiting the willingness and effort to participate wholeheartedly in the activities in chapter 4.

Rubric C differs from the first two sample rubrics in that the teacher's assessment is focused on the extent to which the entire class has achieved a multicultural outcome. The descriptors are easily observable behavior and allow for a range of performance, thus focusing on quality in addition to quantity of content. This rubric can be administered directly following the lesson, during the self-reflection question asked at the end of individual or peer activities, or after the group discussion segment. Based on the results, a decision can be made to repeat the activity with future classes or to expand or modify the content to better meet the outcome.

Student journals can also be used to collect data on the progress of student learning. Information collected from journals reveals the individual's perceptions and feelings about participating in the physical activity. Students should be asked to record their feelings at regular intervals. Although ranging in depth of self-reflection, the information contains results that are not evident through observation. The information can also be recorded on index cards if journals are not available. The results from this tactic can be used at the end of each school's ranking period for a summary analysis.

SAMPLE RUBRIC A Assessing Individual Interaction With a Peer or Partner

Teacher's name: ______________________

Student's name: ______________________

Class period: ______________

Grade: ______________

Date: ______________

ACTUAL SCORE

	4	3	2	1
	EXCELLENT INTERACTION — Always	GOOD INTERACTION — Usually	SOMEWHAT INTERACTIVE — Sometimes	POOR INTERACTION — Needs to be asked or does not exhibit appropriate behavior
	Circle the appropriate number for each criteria			
The student's willingness to select a partner for peer practice sessions	4	3	2	1
The student's willingness to encourage a partner to verbalize his or her opinion	4	3	2	1
The student's willingness to respond to a partner without ridiculing his or her ideas	4	3	2	1
The student's willingness to be tolerant of a partner's limitation	4	3	2	1
The student's willingness to be attentive and courteous to a partner to whom he or she asks questions	4	3	2	1
The student's willingness to assist his or her partner in the organization and execution of the activity	4	3	2	1
The student's willingness to adjust his or her own interests to accommodate a partner's needs	4	3	2	1
The student's willingness to observe his or her partner's ability and offer praise when appropriate	4	3	2	1
The student's willingness to demonstrate cooperative gestures with a partner	4	3	2	1
The student's willingness to work with different partners	4	3	2	1

SAMPLE RUBRIC B Assessing a Student's Group Interactive Skills

Teacher's name: ______________________

Student's name: ______________________

Class period: ____________

Grade: ____________

Date: ____________

ACTUAL SCORE

	4	3	2	1
	EXCELLENT INTERACTION — Always	GOOD INTERACTION — Usually	SOMEWHAT INTERACTIVE — Sometimes	POOR INTERACTION — Needs to be prompted
	Circle the appropriate number for each criteria			
The student's willingness to encourage group members to participate in new or unfamiliar physical education activities	4	3	2	1
The student's willingness to participate in group physical education activities common to different cultures	4	3	2	1
The student's willingness to caution group members not to perform activities beyond their capabilities	4	3	2	1
The student's willingness to involve all group members in the activity	4	3	2	1
The student's willingness to freely seek help from group members	4	3	2	1
The student's willingness to assist group members in performing the assigned activity	4	3	2	1
The student's willingness to modify or change some rules so that other students can fully participate	4	3	2	1
The student's willingness to congratulate group members for the successful completion of the activity	4	3	2	1
The student's willingness to participate in all forums	4	3	2	1
The student's willingness to socially interact with group members after the completion of the activity	4	3	2	1

SAMPLE RUBRIC C Assessing the Extent to Which a Multicultural Outcome Has Been Achieved

Teacher's name: ______________________

Date: ________ Class period: ______ Grade: ______

Title of activity: ______________________

Outcome corresponding with activity: ______________________

____

	5	4	3	2	1
	OUTSTANDING 90-100% of the students achieved the outcome	EXCELLENT 80-89% of the students achieved the outcome	GOOD 70-79% of the students achieved the outcome	POOR 50-69% of the students achieved the outcome	NOT ACHIEVED Less than 50% achievement
	Circle the appropriate number for each criteria				
The class was attentive and listened to the teacher's introduction (i.e., history and origin) of the activity.	5	4	3	2	1
The class demonstrated an eagerness to follow the activity's essential rules for play.	5	4	3	2	1
The class completed either a peer practice session or used a forum for more effective play.	5	4	3	2	1
The class maintained a high level of participation and desire to perform skills.	5	4	3	2	1
The class displayed cooperative gestures before and after the activity.	5	4	3	2	1
Individuals exhibited good self-worth.	5	4	3	2	1
Group work resulted in feelings of pride or accomplishment.	5	4	3	2	1

Teacher's Reflection: ______________________

____

____

CHAPTER

6

Additional Curriculum Considerations

THE NATIONAL ASSOCIATION FOR SPORT AND PHYSICAL EDUCATION CONTENT STANDARDS

No contemporary teacher education document in physical education can be complete without acknowledging the importance of NASPE content standards (1995) and identifying how the information reflects those standards. While this document used the standards as a guideline in the decision to select each activity, clearly the greatest attention focused on content standards 5, 6, and 7 as identified below:

A physically educated person

1. Demonstrates competency in many movement forms and proficiency in a few movement forms.
2. Applies movement concepts and principles to the forming and development of motor skills.
3. Exhibits a physically active lifestyle.
4. Achieves and maintains a health-enhancing level of physical fitness.
5. ☆ Demonstrates responsible personal and social behavior in physical activity settings.
6. ☆ Demonstrates understanding and respect for differences among people in physical activity settings.
7. ☆ Understands that physical activity provides opportunities for enjoyment, challenge, self-expression, and social interaction.

MAKING USE OF COGNATES

There are numerous words similar to English in translation and pronunciation from many languages. Knowledge of these words assists the teacher who has resorted to only using hand signals and demonstrations. For example, for communicating to students from Spain, some analogous words include sport *(recreación)*, move forward *(avanzar)*, purpose *(proponer)*, join *(juntar)*, and protect *(proteccion)*. Examples of Italian words include sport *(gli sport)*, partner *(associato)*, guard *(guardare)*, group *(gruppo)*, and passing *(passeggero)*. Words from French include sport *(le sport)*, finish *(finir)*, paddles *(les raquettes)*, signals *(signalisation)*, walk *(marcher)*, and carry *(porter)*. It is also important to note that many words depicting shapes and forms are very similar in numerous languages and may be used to structure practice formations. Examples include *circle* (English), *el circulo* (Spanish), *cerchio* (Italian), and *le cercle* (French). Likewise, students can be asked to practice skills in triangular formations (e.g., *el triangulo* (Spanish), *triangolo* (Italian), and *le triangle* (French)). The names of particular sports are also very similar among countries. See box below.

EXAMPLES OF NAME SIMILARITIES IN SPORT

UNITED STATES	SPAIN	ITALY	FRANCE
cycling	el ciclismo	il ciclismo	le cyclisme
baseball	el béisbol	il baseball	le base-ball
skiing	el esquí	lo sci	le ski
tennis	el tenis	il tennis	le tennis
judo	el judo	il judo	le judo
gymnastics	la gimnasia	la ginnastica	la gymnastique

INTERNATIONAL SKILL PRACTICE FORMATIONS

Many of the activities included in this resource contain motor skills that are unfamiliar to students. The following formations have a long history of existence in countries throughout the world. They are presented as a means for the teacher to have all students practice a throwing, catching, or kicking skill in order to enhance their performance during game play. They are not intended as a substitute for peer practice, unless the teacher's lack of equipment necessitates larger group practice situations.

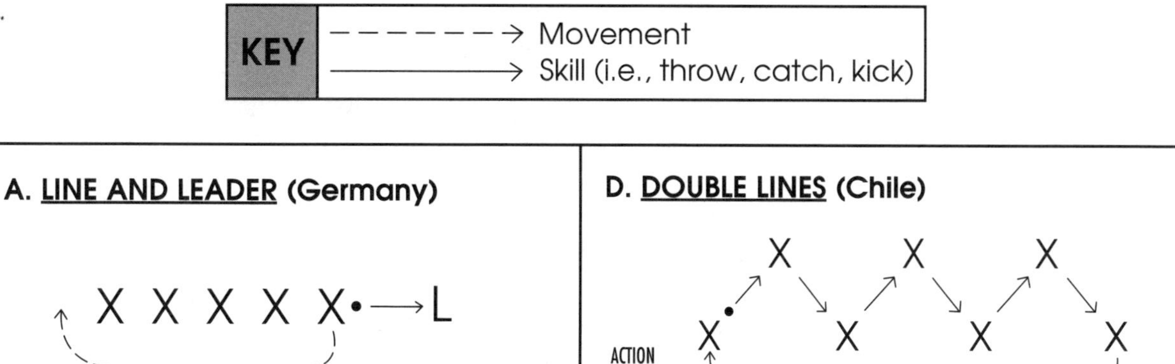

A. LINE AND LEADER (Germany)

Student moves to the end of the line after the skill (e.g., throw) is performed. The leader remains stationary.

B. LINE AND LEADER VARIATION (Denmark)

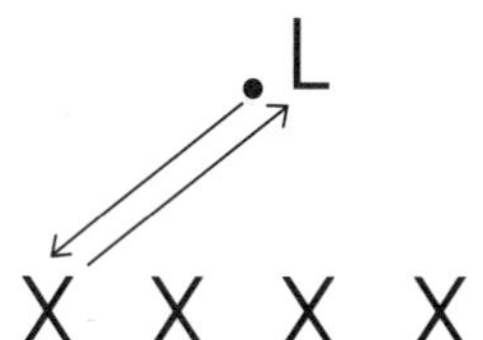

All students and the leader remain stationary. Leader throws to first student who throws back to the leader.

C. CIRCLE AND LEADER (Columbia)

All students remain stationary. After the leader throws to all students, he or she switches places with a circle player.

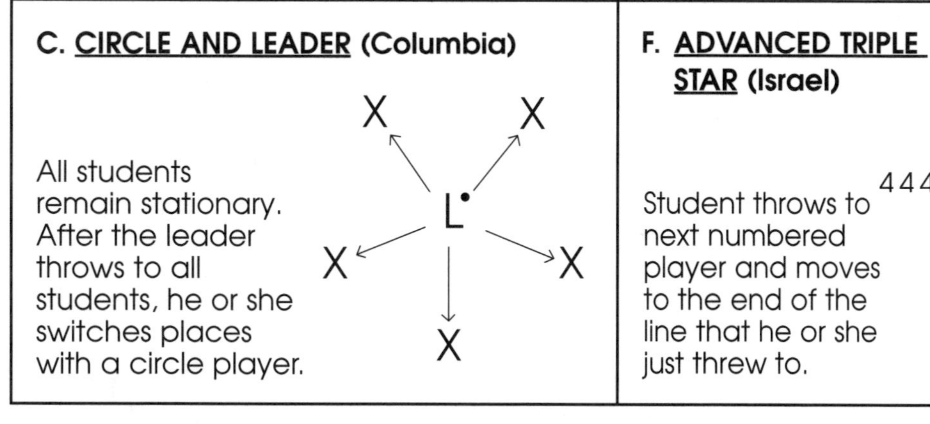

D. DOUBLE LINES (Chile)

Students throw to the end of the line where the last player runs to the first position and all players advance to the next space.

E. STAR (USA)

Students throw in a star formation.

F. ADVANCED TRIPLE STAR (Israel)

Student throws to next numbered player and moves to the end of the line that he or she just threw to.

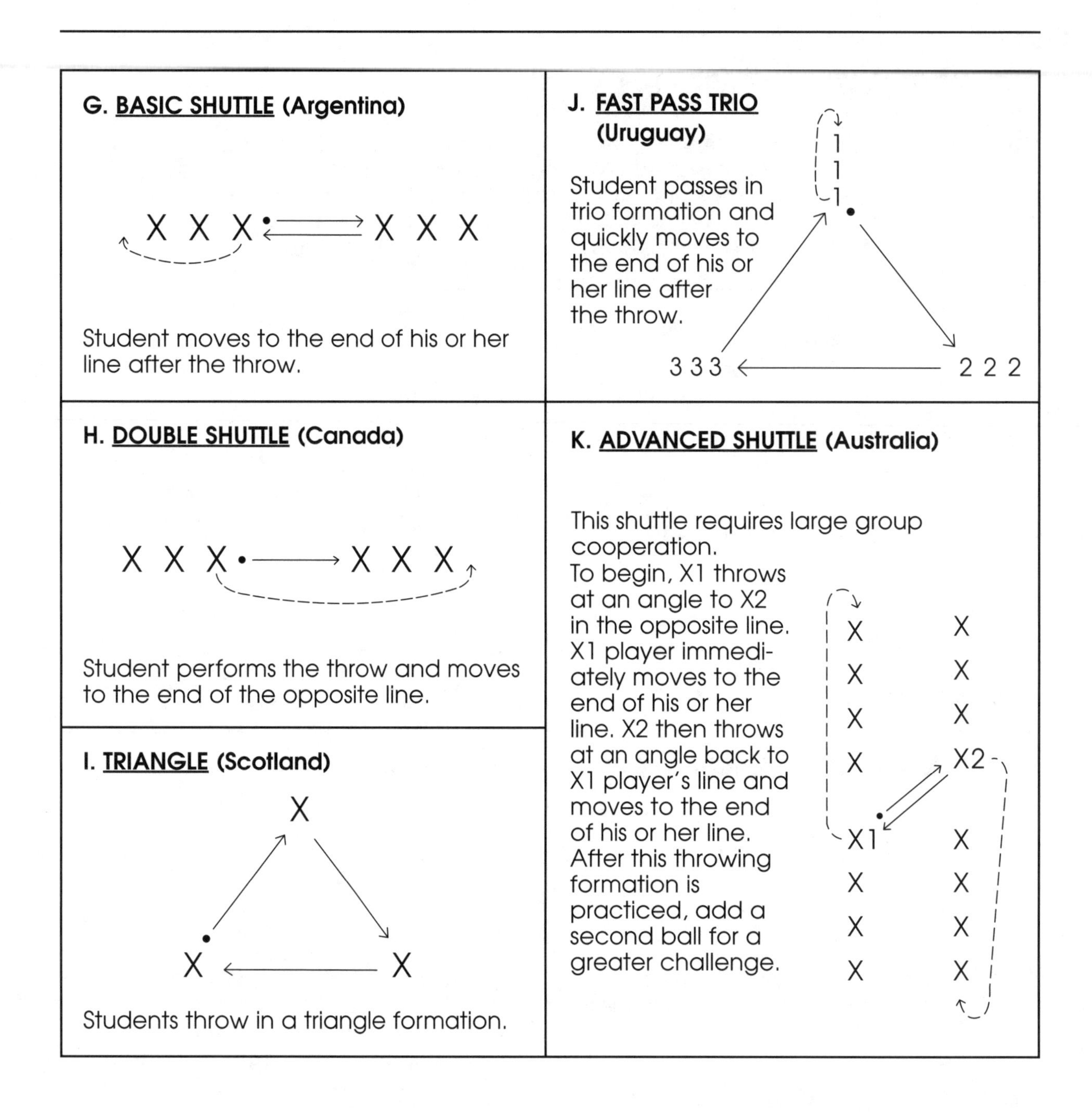
G. BASIC SHUTTLE (Argentina)
X X X X X X
Student moves to the end of his or her line after the throw.
J. FAST PASS TRIO (Uruguay)
Student passes in trio formation and quickly moves to the end of his or her line after the throw.
1 1 1
3 3 3
2 2 2
H. DOUBLE SHUTTLE (Canada)
X X X X X X
Student performs the throw and moves to the end of the opposite line.
I. TRIANGLE (Scotland)
X
X X
Students throw in a triangle formation.
K. ADVANCED SHUTTLE (Australia)
This shuttle requires large group cooperation.
To begin, X1 throws at an angle to X2 in the opposite line. X1 player immediately moves to the end of his or her line. X2 then throws at an angle back to X1 player's line and moves to the end of his or her line. After this throwing formation is practiced, add a second ball for a greater challenge.
X X
X X
X X
X X2
X1 X
X X
X X
X X

BULLETIN BOARD SAYINGS THAT PROMOTE INTERPERSONAL RELATIONSHIPS

We share the earth!

Be just as enthusiastic about the success of others
as you are about your own!

To be happy, you must forget yourself!

It is not how much we have, but how much we enjoy!

Anything is within your reach!

You have only failed when you have failed to try!

Enjoy learning new things, reading new books, thinking new thoughts!

Accept life's challenges with a friend!

It is more important to be human than to be important!

Discover your interests, potentials, and talents with a friend!

We're all in this together!

People are divided into three groups: those who make things happen,
those who watch things happen, and those who wonder what happened!

It is amazing how much can be accomplished if no one cares who gets the credit!

Sometimes you have to be silent to be heard!

Most problems are really the absence of ideas!

No act of kindness, no matter how small, is ever wasted!

There are no problems, only solutions!

The past is my heritage, the present is my responsibility,
the future is my challenge!

To share with a friend is to see twice the beauty!

Forget the misgivings in your past and
move on to greater achievements in the future!

Skool is Kool!

"HELLO" FROM AROUND THE WORLD

Australia, South Africa, New Zealand, USA, UK, Canada, Ireland - ***Hello***

Denmark - ***Goddag***

Egypt - ***Ahlan Wasahlan***

Finland - ***Hyvaa Paivaa***

France - ***Bonjour***

Germany - ***Guten Tag***

Greece - ***Kalimera***

Iceland - ***Godan Daginn***

India - ***Namaskar***

Italy - ***Buongiorno***

Japan - ***Konnichiwa***

Norway - ***Go Day***

Poland - ***Dzien Dobry***

Portugal - ***Bom Dia***

Russia - ***Zdravstvuyite***

Spain - ***Buenos Dias***

Sweden - ***God Dag***

Turkey - ***Iya Gunler***

Zulu - ***Kunjani***

COUNTRY SYMBOLS FOR TEAMS

Argentina - **Ceiba**

Columbia - **Orchid**

Denmark - **Beech Tree**

England - **Rose**

Greece - **Olive Branch**

Ireland - **Shamrock**

Japan - **Cherry Blossom**

Scotland - **Thistle**

Spain - **Red Carnation**

Turkey - **Tulip**

Bulgaria - **Lion**

China - **Dragon**

India - **Royal Bengal Tiger**

Russia - **Brown Bear**

South Africa - **Blue Crane**

USA - **Bald Eagle**

BIBLIOGRAPHY

Adler, Sol. (1993). *Multicultural Communication Skills in the Classroom.* Needham Heights, MA: Allyn and Bacon.

Anderson, G.F. (1969). *Knowledge and Understanding in Physical Education.* Washington, D.C.: The American Alliance for Health, Physical Education, Recreation, and Dance.

Aponte, J.F., et al. (1995). *Psychological Interventions and Cultural Diversity.* Needham Heights, MA: Allyn and Bacon.

Baker, G.C. (1994). *Planning and Organizing for Multicultural Instruction.* Menlo Park, CA: Addison-Wesley.

Banks, J.A. (1997). *Educating Citizens in a Multicultural Society.* New York: Teachers College Press.

Banks, J.A., et al. (1995). *Handbook of Research on Multicultural Education.* New York: Macmillan.

Banks, J.A. (1999). *An Introduction to Multicultural Education, (2nd ed.).* Needham Heights, MA: Allyn and Bacon.

Banks, J.A. and Banks, C.A.M. (eds). (1997). *Multicultural Education: Issues and Perspectives, (3rd ed.).* Needham Heights, MA: Allyn and Bacon.

Banks, J.A. (1994). *Multiethnic Education: Theory and Practice, (3rd ed.).* Needham Heights, MA: Allyn and Bacon.

Banks, J.A. (1997). *Teaching Strategies for Ethnic Studies, (6th ed.).* Boston, MA: Allyn and Bacon.

Baruth, L.G. and Manning, M.L. (1992). *Multicultural Education of Children and Adolescents.* Needham Heights, MA: Allyn and Bacon.

Battle Vold, E. (ed). (1992). *Multicultural education in early childhood classrooms.* National Education Association.

Bennett, C.I. (1995). *Comprehensive multicultural education: Theory and practice, (3rd ed.).* Needham Heights, MA: Allyn and Bacon.

Benson, S. (1981). *Ambiguous Ethnicity.* Cambridge: Cambridge University Press.

Bullard, S. (1991, December). Sorting through the multicultural rhetoric. *Educational Leadership.* 49(4), 4-7.

Butt, K.L. and Pahnos, M. (1995). Why we need a multicultural focus in our schools. *JOPERD,* 66(1), 48-53.

Campbell, D.E. (2000). *Choosing Democracy: A Practical Guide for Multicultural Education, (2nd ed.).* Columbus, OH: Merrill.

Carger, C.L. (1996). *Of Borders and Dreams: A Mexican-American Experience of Urban Education.* New York: Teachers College Press.

Clegg, L.B., Miller, E., and Vanderhoof, Jr., W. (1995). *Celebrating Diversity: A Multicultural Resource.* Albany, NY: Delmar.

Crawford, L.W. (1993). *Language and Literacy Learning in Multicultural Classrooms.* Needham Heights, MA: Allyn and Bacon.

Cummins, J. and Sayers, D. (1995). *Brave New Schools: Challenging Cultural Literacy Through Global Learning Networks.* New York: St. Martin's Press.

Davidman, L. and Davidman, P.T. (1997). *Teaching with a Multicultural Perspective: A Practical Guide, (2nd ed.).* New York: Longman.

DeGaetano, Y., Williams, L.R., and Volk, D. (1998). *Kaleidoscope: A Multicultural Approach for the Primary School Classroom.* Columbus, OH: Merrill.

Dentler, R.A. and Halfner, A.L. (1997). *Hosting Newcomers.* New York: Teachers College Press.

DeVillar, R.A., Faltis, C.J., and Cummins, J.P. (eds.). (1994). *Cultural Diversity in Schools: From Rhetoric to Practice.* State University of New York Press.

Diaz, C. (1992). *Multicultural Education for the 21st Century.* Washington, DC: NEA.

Diaz, C.F., et al. (1999). *Global Perspectives for Educators.* Needham Heights, MA: Allyn and Bacon.

Dilg, M. (1999). *Race and Culture in the Classroom.* New York: Teachers College Press.

Dinnerstein, L., Nichols, R.L., and Reimers, D.M. (1996). *Natives and Strangers: A Multicultural History of Americans.* New York: Oxford University Press.

Donnelly, R.J., Helms, W.G., & Mitchell, E.D. (1958). *Active Games and Contests, (2nd ed.).* New York: Ronald Press.

Dunne, R.S. and Griggs, S.A. (1995). *Multiculturalism and Learning Style: Teaching and Counseling Adolescents.* Wesport, CT: Praeger Publishing.

Faltis, C.J. (1997). *Joinfostering: Adapting Teaching Strategies for the Multilingual Classroom, (2nd ed.).* Columbus, OH: Merrill.

Farrell, E. (1990). *Hanging In and Dropping Out: Voice of At-Risk High School Students.* New York: Teachers College Press.

Fisher, S.N. and Ochsenwald, W. (1990). *The Middle East: A History, (4th ed.).* New York: McGraw-Hill.

Fu, V. and Stremmel, A. (1999). *Affirming Democracy Through Democratic Conversation.* Columbus, OH: Merrill.

Garcia, E. (1994). *Understanding and Meeting the Challenge of Student Cultural Diversity.* Boston: Houghton Mifflin.

Garcia, J.G. and Zea, M.C. (1997). *Psychological Interventions and Research with Latino Populations.* Needham Heights, MA: Allyn and Bacon.

Gollnick, D.M. and Chinn, P.C. (1998). *Multicultural Education in a Pluralistic Society, (5th ed.).* Columbus, OH: Merrill.

Grant, C.A. and Gomez, M.L. (eds.). (1996). *Making Schools Multicultural: Campus and Classroom.* Columbus, OH: Merrill.

Grant, C.A. (ed.). (1995). *Educating For Diversity.* Needham Heights, MA: Allyn and Bacon.

Grant, C.A. (ed.). (1992). *Research and Multicultural Education: From the Margins to the Mainstream.* London: Falmer Press.

Grant, C. and Sleeter, C. (1998). *Turning on Learning, (2nd ed.).* Columbus, OH: Merrill.

Grossman, H. (1995). *Teaching in a Diverse Society.* Needham Heights, MA: Allyn and Bacon.

Grossman, H. and Grossman, S.H. (1994). *Gender Issues in Education.* Needham Heights, MA: Allyn and Bacon.

Hall, P. (ed.). (1997). *Race Ethnicity and Multiculturalism.* Hamdon, CT: Garland Publishing.

Harris, P.R. and Mohan, R.T. (1987). *Managing Cultural Differences.* Houston, TX: Gulf.

Hawley, W.D. and Jackson, A.W. (eds). (1995). *Toward a Common Destiny: Improving Race and Ethnic Relations in America.* San Francisco: Jossey-Bass.

Hernandez, H. (2000). *Multicultural Education: A Teacher's Guide to Content and Process, (2nd ed.).* Upper Saddle River, NJ: Prentice-Hall.

Hollins, E.R. (ed.). (1995). *Transforming Curriculum for a Culturally Diverse Society.* Mahwah, NJ: Lawrence Erlbaum Associates.

Howell, M.L. and Phillips, M. (1997). *Sports and Games.* New York: Time-Life Books.

Howell, R., Howell, M.L., Toohey, D.P., and Toohey, D.M. (1979). *Methodology in Comparative Physical Education and Sport.* Champaign, IL: Stipes Publishing.

Hunt, S.E. and Cain, E. (1941). *Games: The World Around.* New York: A.S. Barnes.

Hutchinson, G.E. (1995). Gender-fair teaching in physical education. *JOPERD,* 66(1), 42-47.

King, S. (1994). Winning the race against racism. *JOPERD,* 65(9), 69-74.

Kizer, D.L., Piper, D.L. and Santer, W.E. (1984). *A Practical Approach to Teaching Physical Education.* New York: Monument Publication.

Ladson-Billings, G. (1997). *The Dreamkeepers: Successful Teachers of African American Children.* San Francisco: Jossey-Bass.

Lee, S.J. (1996). *Unraveling the "Model Minority" Stereotype: Listening to Asian American Youth.* New York: Teachers College Press.

Li, M.H. and Li, P. (1990). *Understanding Asian Americans: A Curriculum Resource Guide.* New York: Neal-Schuman.

Lucas, S.R. (1999). *Tracking Inequality: Stratification and Mobility in American High Schools.* New York: Teachers College Press.

Manning, M.L. and Baruth, L.G. (1996). *Multicultural Education of Children and Adolescents, (2nd. ed.).* Boston: Allyn and Bacon.

Manning, M.L. and Baruth, L.G. (1995). *Students at Risk.* Needham Heights, MA: Allyn and Bacon.

McCormick, T.M. (1994). *Creating the Nonsexist Classroom: A Multicultural Approach.* New York: Teachers College Press.

Middlebrooks, S. (1998). *Getting to Know City Kids: Understanding Their Thinking, Imagining and Socializing.* New York: Teachers College Press.

Milberg, A. (1976). *Street Games.* New York: McGraw-Hill.

Miller C.L. and Peacock, T.D. (1998). *Collected Wisdom: American Indian Education.* Needham Heights, MA: Allyn and Bacon.

Miller-Lachman, L. and Taylor, L.S. (1995). *Schools For All: Educating Children in a Diverse Society.* Albany, NY: Delmar.

NASPE. (1995). *Moving Into the Future: National Standards for Physical Education - A Guide to Content and Assessment.* St. Louis, MO: Mosby.

Nieto, S. (1996). *Affirming Diversity: The Sociological Context of Multicultural Education, (2nd ed.).* White Plains, NY: Longman.

Nieto, S. (2000). *Affirming Diversity: The Sociological Context of Multicultural Education, (3rd ed.).* White Plains, NY: Longman.

Omi, M. (1994). *Racial Formation in the United States: 1960-1990.* New York: Routledge.

Orlando, L. (1993). *The Multicultural Game Book: More Than 70 Traditional Games from 30 Countries/Grades 1-6.* New York: Scholastic Professional Books.

Pedersen, P. and Carey, J. C. (1994). *Multicultural Counseling in Schools: A Practical Handbook.* Needham Heights, MA: Allyn and Bacon.

Phelan, P. and Davidson, A.L. (eds.). (1993). *Renegotiating Cultural Diversity in American Schools.* New York: Teachers College Press.

Phillips, J.H. and Carter, J.L. (1985, January). "Tired of being chosen last? Humanistic alternatives to group division." *Journal of Physical Education, Recreation, and Dance,* 56(1), 96-97.

Placek, J. and Giffin, P. (1983). *Fair Play in the Gym: Race and Sex Equity in Physical Education.* Amherst, MA: The Network.

Powell, R.R., Zehm, S., and Garcia, J. (1996). *Field Experience: Strategies for Exploring Diversity in the Schools.* Columbus, OH: Merrill.

Putnam, J. (1997). *Cooperative Learning in Diverse Classrooms.* Columbus, OH: Merrill.

Redman, G.L. (1999). *A Casebook for Exploring Diversity in K-12 Classrooms.* Columbus, OH: Merrill.

Rendon, L.I., Holpe, R.O., and Associates. (1995). *Educating a New Majority: Transforming America's Educational System for Diversity.* San Francisco: Jossey-Bass.

Renyi, J. (1993). *Going Public: Schooling for a Diverse Democracy.* New York: New Press.

Schofield, J.W. (1989). *Black and White in School.* New York: Teachers College Press.

Schniedewind, N., and Davidson, E. (1998). *Open Minds to Equality: A Sourcebook of Learning Activities to Affirm Diversity and Promote Equality, (2nd ed.).* Needham Heights, MA: Allyn and Bacon.

Segall, W., and Wilson, A.V. (1998). *Introduction to Education: Teaching in a Diverse Society.* Needham Heights, MA: Allyn and Bacon.

Siccone, F. (1995). *Celebrating Diversity: Building Self-Esteem in Today's Multicultural Classrooms.* Needham Heights, MA: Allyn and Bacon.

Sill, G.M. and Chaplin, M.T. (1993). O*pening the American Mind: Race Ethnicity and Gender in Higher Education.* Newark, DE: University of Delaware Press.

Sleeter, C.E. and Grant, C.A. (1999). *Making Choices for Multicultural Education: Five Approaches to Race, Class and Gender, (3rd ed.).* Columbus, OH: Merrill.

Sparks, III, W.G. (1994). Culturally responsive pedagogy: A framework for addressing multicultural issues. *JOPERD,* 65(9), 33-36, 61.

Stanley, L.S. (1995). Multicultural questions, action research answers. *Quest,* 47, 19-33.

Stephan, S. (1999). *Reducing Prejudice and Stereotyping in Schools.* New York: Teachers College Press.

Swisher, K. and Swisher, C. (1986). A multicultural physical education approach. *JOPERD,* 57(7), 35-39.

Torbet, M. and Schnieder, L.B. (1986). Positive multicultural interaction: Using low organized games. *JOPERD,* 57(7), 40-44.

Tiedt, P.L. and Tiedt, I.M. (1999). *Multicultural Teaching: A Handbook of Activities, Information and Resources, (5th ed.).* Needham Heights, MA: Allyn and Bacon.

Vargas, L.A. and Koss-Chiono, J.D. (eds.). (1992). *Working with Culture.* San Francisco: Jossey-Bass.

Vicker, J.N. (1990). *Instructional Design for Teaching Physical Activities: A Knowledge Structures Approach.* Champaign, IL: Human Kinetics.

Vinton, I. (1970). *The Folkways Omnibus of Children's Games.* Harrisburg, PA: Stackpole Books.

Walker-Moffat, W. (1995). *The Other Side of the Asian American Success Story.* San Francisco: Jossey-Bass.

Wax, M.L. (1993). How culture misdirects multiculturalism. *Anthropology and Educational Quarterly.* 24(2), 99-115

Wessinger, N.P. (1994). Celebrating our differences – Fostering ethnicity in homogenous settings. *JOPERD,* 65(9), 62-68.

Wlodkowski, R.J. and Ginsberg, M.B. (1995). *Diversity and Motivation: Culturally Responsive Teaching.* San Francisco: Jossey-Bass.

Wright, G. (1978). *Rand McNally Illustrated Dictionary of Sports.* Chicago: Rand McNally.

Yeo, F.L. (1997). *Inner-City Schools, Multiculturalism, and Teacher Education: A Professional Journey.* Hamdon, CT: Garland Publishing.

Yetman, N. (ed.). (1999). *Majority and Minority: The Dynamics of Race and Ethnicity in American Life, (6th ed.).* Needham Heights, MA: Allyn and Bacon.

Zogby, J.G. (1990). *Arab American Today: A Demographic Profile of Arab Americans.* Washington, DC: Arab American Institute.

ABOUT THE AUTHORS

Rhonda Clements, EdD, is the author of eight books on movement, play, and games. She is the president of the American Association for the Child's Right to Play, a UN-recognized association composed of experts in play, games, and sports in 49 other countries. The program's primary purpose is to protect, preserve, and promote play and leisure activities throughout the world.

Dr. Clements has written more than 70 articles related to physical education (including 20 on sport and play factors) and has been interviewed by more than 200 journalists regarding children's right to leisure and physical play. She is also a consultant for numerous toy manufactures that use her expertise in physical activity and manipulative playthings. She has presented at 20 international conferences on topics related to cultural understanding though play and sport.

Dr. Clements is a professor and the coordinator of graduate physical education at Hofstra University in Long Island, New York, where she conducts research and teaches about historical and sociocultural issues in sport and physical education. In her leisure time, she enjoys world travel; historical museums; race walking; and collecting antiquarian books on teacher training, games, and sport. She lives in New York City.

A licensed physical educator with experience in both the public and the private sectors, **Suzanne K. Kinzler, MS,** has taught in a multicultural environment for more than 12 years. She was a key writer on the assessment portion of the New York City Board of Education Physical Education Committee and she is a member of the American Alliance for Health, Physical Education, Recreation and Dance; the American Association for the Child's Right to Play; and the Women's Sport Foundation.

Kinzler is a physical education and health instructor at Queens Gateway to the Health Sciences Secondary School in Jamaica, New York. The mother of two boys, Kinzler is an avid reader who enjoys curriculum development, creative movement, dancing, and fitness walking. She lives in Woodmere, New York.